THAT'S MY BUSINESS

Edited by

Brian Lewis and Jo Edge

YORKSHIRE ART CIRCUS
1990

Published by Yorkshire Art Circus,
School Lane, Glasshoughton,
Castleford, West Yorkshire WF10 4QH
Telephone (0977) 550401

Typsetting and Printing: FM Repro Ltd., Repro House, 69 Lumb Lane
Roberttown, Liversedge, West Yorkshire WF15 7NB

ISBN 0 947780 61 0

Yorkshire Art Circus is a unique book publisher. We link our books with performances and exhibitions and offer workshops for the first time writer. Yorkshire Art Circus projects have successfully toured community centres, colleges, galleries, clubs, galas and art centres. In all our work we bring new artists to new audiences.

For details of our programme of performances, exhibitions, conferences and workshops send for our brochure and book list at the address above.

Yorkshire Art Circus is a non-profitmaking limited company.

We would like to thank the following people and organisations for the use of their photographs:

Wakefield Metropolitan District Council
Pontefract and Castleford Express
Stephen McClarence
Kevin Reynolds
Mike Petty

CONTENTS

We would like to thank the following people who have contributed to this book:

Alice Chapman
Tommy Doughty
May Kirk
Audrey Haggerty
Annie Lyman
Kathryn Swift
Catherine Trevor
Karen Byford
Pauline Wigglesworth
Linda McGillivray
Barbara Stewart
Andrew Godley
Ben Kellett
Brian Caswell
Ethel Weatherhill
Valerie Fairbanks
John Ladley
Jack Gonek
Amanda Spalding
Joan Thornton
Joanne Thornton
Paul Thornton
Mr. Groves
Jay Earle
Barry Brake
Ian Taylor
Dave Cope
John Gummerson
George Kelly
Sue Stirk
Abdulmajid Rakhada
Tony Morgan
Peter Downham
Jackie Downham
Edward France
Geoff Leighton
Richard Newman
Hassan Nejatpour
Hugh Morley
Janet Edgar
Vicky Foxton
Peter Clay
Jane Hollowday
Rachel Van Riel
Lorraine Garbutt
Chris Hesketh
Gill Grennell
Lee Gilbert
Paul Tully
Amanda Casberry
Susan Hitchcock
Derek Hitchcock
Ron Morris
Beverley de Whytell
Eric Wilkinson
Julie Birch
Mike Birch
Arthur Crossfield
Margaret Crossfield
James Goff
Marjorie Wood
Judi Alston
Pat Smith
Stuart Kelly
Ian Johnstone
Ian Hall
Vera Parkin
Graham Poulter
Dave Foster
Mike Petty

Editorial Team:

Lilian Whiteley
Tony Lumb
Rachel Van Riel
Janet Spears
Rachel Adam
Reini Schühle
Margaret Edwards
Ian Clayton
Karen Byford
John Ladley

INTRODUCTION

The problem with this book is that there is a story on every street corner and most of them deserve to be printed. The majority of people have been involved in a business at some time and have a story to tell. There are black economy stories, accounts of trying to set up evening businesses, anecdotes about junk stalls and ones about ventures which went astray because of lack of finance or forward planning. You have only to stand at the counter, in the workshop or sit with a local government official involved in job creation for the stories to flow. In the end you begin to recognise that you could go on collecting for ever and still find more and more interesting tales.

We went out into the community and asked questions because we wanted to know what was learned when you failed or succeeded in business. What emerged was that there was no blue print for success, on the other hand if you listened carefully the anecdotes were instructive. We believe that if you understand decision making processes you have more control over your life and that you learn these skills by hearing about the experiences of others.

This is not a handbook about how to manage a business but anyone who reads it will benefit. When you read about a man who built from scratch a business with a turnover of £55,000,000 or listen to what a nineteen year old woman is saying about planning, it is the similarities which strike you and not the differences.

A number of people have helped with this book. We would particularly like to thank our colleagues in the Art Circus Education team: Janet Spears, Margaret Edwards, Lilian Whiteley and Tony Lumb. Between them they had an encyclopaedic knowledge of the local area and when a new principle emerged would go out into the community and find a story which illustrated it. We would also like to thank the photographers Stephen McClarence, Kevin Reynolds and Mike Petty. Also Richard Van Riel, of Pontefract Museum, for his knowledge of the area and use of Wakefield MDC (Leisure Services) photographic collection.

Stephen McClarence

Who wants to be a millionaire?
I do

WHO WANTS TO BE A MILLIONAIRE?

Setting Up

If you've got the brass go for gold

☐ It's exciting creating something from nothing especially when there's a chance to make lots of money. I suppose it is the unpredictability that I like. On the other hand the idea can be a little frightening if, like me, you have been brought up with non-risk takers, other people's employees. I'm not naive, I know that I can go bankrupt and that can be humiliating.

☐ It's very easy to get carried away with the excitement but going into business is not a fantasy, it is very much a reality, a big responsibility and a gamble. Any debts accrued by the business are a personal liability and therefore not to be taken lightly. Always remember the business comes first, and in the initial stages you have to put up with long working hours, no holiday, not even proper weekends. There's no such thing as a friend in business, at the best everyone becomes a colleague. Sacrifices have to be made in order to achieve success.

☐ Give me moments back and one I would choose was travelling as my own boss in a hired van full of arts magazines moving towards Whitby. The patch I would like to be on is that flat bit after you rise up from Fylingdale, the bit where the sheep stray onto the road. The radio would be on and someone, possibly Bing Crosby would be singing "I'm busy doing nothing, working the whole day through."

☐ I started twenty odd years ago working an on-the-side job retailing washing-up liquid from a room in Wheldon Lane, Castleford. Now the company which has my name on its notepaper has a turnover of £55,000,000. At first I did everything: wrote copy, mixed the ingredients in a 50 gallon drum, packaged it and hawked it in a van to housewives within a five mile radius of my base. Now I do not handle any day-to-day business. My job is to look to strategic planning. There's a new communications revolution coming and I need to understand it, and because I have the capacity to stand back, I think that I do. If my car breaks down tonight I can't get it going, but I know how to get someone who can. On the other hand I do understand the principles of the petrol engine.

☐ Forget self-pity. If you've got the brass, go for gold. All you need is courage, patience and intelligence, but don't jump in the bath without testing the water. The business world is a shark-infested sea waiting for the uninitiated, so tread bravely but use caution. Your brain runs on high octane fuel: so use it or waste it, you have the choice.

Research the market; become an investigative journalist and ask questions, a lot of questions. Make a nuisance of yourself in your thirst for knowledge. If you know of ten shops selling unisex underwear, make an appointment and visit them all. Write out a questionnaire of what you would like to know and take it with you. This is professional etiquette, so deal professionally with professional people. That saves time; theirs, which they'll appreciate, and yours. Be prepared — count your chickens before they hatch or you might end up with egg on your face.

Modern methods are needed to meet the needs of modern society, so is acquisition and application of sound business sense. If you haven't got it, get it. Don't live in a closet. Advice, help and counselling are readily to hand. Don't send horror stories to Mills and Boon. Know the market and target it. Survival is the embryo of success. Aim to keep your head above water during the first twelve months and be prepared to make sacrifices to meet demands and deadlines.

☐ I often ask myself why, after twenty years of working for a good wage, in a reliable and interesting job, did I give it all up to start my own business? Most certainly I would have been better off financially if I had stayed working for someone else. But I would have missed out on a very important part of my life; a life which was to change in every way. I chose to become not a small cog in a big wheel, but a cog without a wheel.

☐ Establish contacts when, where and how you can. If a posh dinner and a bottle of plonk land a contract then it's money well spent. Be polite and a good listener. Small or large? Size is unimportant. Join forces with a friend if needs be. Two heads are better than one. Prepare to learn from your own mistakes. Be diplomatic yet positive in bargaining. Obviously there will be tears but the consequence of a dented ego is the voice of experience.

Finally remember, many business acquaintances are intelligent, inquisitive and interesting. Are you?

☐ I believe that nobody is put on earth to be a collier or a builder or what have you. You can adapt, be what you decide to be, but if you look round here you might not think so. I went straight into the pits like most of my school mates and just like the rest of them I'd been bred to it and it was expected that that was it until retirement. I hadn't done very well at school, I was good at sums, but poor at writing and I didn't get helped; well they don't bother with the slow ones do they? I stayed down the pit for just a few years and I hated every bit of the time I was down. I couldn't wait for Fridays and holidays. In 1968 I decided I'd had enough and packed in to set up in scrap.

Bear in mind that there was no such thing as redundancy at that time, not like now, it was very unfashionable to leave the security of a pit job. All my mates laughed at me, said I'd be back within a month, but that made me even more determined, I've got my pride. After I'd done the scrap for a bit I decided to go into road haulage and everybody laughed at me again. I suppose they'd a right to because I'd no experience whatsoever, anyhow my wife borrowed £150 from the bank because I didn't have an account and lent it to me. With that I bought a second hand little truck and that was that.

I've never looked back. I ended up where I employed ten men and I had wagons going right up to 32 ton articulated lorries. And do you know, I never bought a lorry if I didn't have enough in the bank to cover it; prudence was my rule right from the very beginning and it's stood me in good stead.

Another rule I made was to ask whenever I didn't know. When I made my first haulage trip I didn't even know how to rope and sheet a load. I turned to this other driver and asked how to do it. He thought I was kidding him, but I explained that it was my first time and he willingly showed me how to carry on, folding the sheets and what have you. And that's how you learn, I've only to be shown once and then I know because I've got a good instinct. Different from my schooldays; when there's twenty or more in a class you don't have to listen, but when you're on your own you have to do. Watching people and a good instinct has helped me get on. I can look at a job now and study it for a bit then tell you exactly what kind of truck you need. Same if I hear a truck going past, I could probably tell you what kind of engine it's got in it. That comes with practice.

☐ Running a small business has made me change my idea of wealth. We teeter on the edge of financial disaster every week because so much depends on whether a customer is going to pay up on time. My idea of wealth is to have both the fridge and the freezer full.

Stephen McClarence

Not frightened by risk

☐ I've gone through life laughing and I know I wouldn't make a business man, I wouldn't want the anxiety. It would change me. When I stop laughing I want to die.

☐ Personal contact is important to me. I did think about becoming a driving examiner, but you have to be so distant with people, inhuman really, it's like sitting there with a fish. Most of my custom comes from word of mouth. We live in a village and I think I've taught most of the village to drive. I taught the mothers and now I'm teaching the children. Some of my clients came with me when I left BSM which was reassuring. I went into business because I used to like driving, but now I'm glad to turn the key off.

☐ The only time I ever consider working for myself is either when I have lost my job or I am fed up and frustrated with the organisation I work for. I have lots of ideas for starting a business and I see a lot of people who are good at it. The biggest problem is that although I like an element of risk in my life, to run your own business involves so many undertakings that the idea frightens me. I suppose it is just a lack of confidence really.

☐ Some people often say that you lose friends when you go into business, but I wonder which friends they mean. I have not lost any true friends and can say truly that I have gained some friends who were former acquaintances. I don't think that I have changed at all since I began, I still go into the local pub and to the rugby matches and keep up my interest in the local scouts. I am the secretary of the local Chamber of Trade in our town. I can only say what has been said many times before, that being my own boss is very self-satisfying, although I have a saying that, "You're never your own boss when dealing with the public."

☐ I had worked for a number of years for a firm of accountants and was quite happy

Stephen McClarence

Stephen McClarence

there, the only drawback was the amount of work I took home to do in my own time for which I received no payment. It was always done as a favour. In the end I decided to go freelance and found I could get as much work as I wanted.

After a time my ex-boss contacted me and asked if I could help out with some urgent work. I agreed and when we discussed my fee he was quite satisfied. We are now in a situation where I do regular work for him, I earn more money than I did as an employee and I have the status of being self-employed. The opposite side of the situation is that I appreciate the stability of working for someone I know and whose methods I am familiar with. All in all it is a very satisfactory arrangement.

☐ People think if you are a 'professional' you have a safe job. I've got a degree and have been working for ten years now. I have been made redundant once and come very close to it a second time. I have never thought seriously about starting my own business because I can't think single-mindedly enough. I belong in public service, serving the wider community and it's difficult to do that running your own business.

☐ If you were bright at Normanton Grammar you got pushed toward subjects like English Literature and so that's what I ended up doing at university. No one sews in our family although from an early age I had spent time buying scraps of cloth from the market and making my own dolls' clothes.

One of the girls I met at university had similar interests and in our final year we took to organising fashion shows in the Union building and making a bit of money that way. Most people from the course decided to go into teaching, journalism or the media, but we went in a totally different direction and applied for a vocational course in London for graduates interested in fashion. You didn't need a degree which was fashion related, the BA(Hons) Literature was enough, but you were required to do extensive aptitude tests. It was a brilliant course.

So, if you ask me why I am here it's because I enjoyed dressing up Cindy dolls as a child.

☐ Even as a child one of my favourite games was mixing mud pies, then baking them in a gap between the top of the air raid shelter door and its covering of corrugated iron and sub soil. So it is to be expected that I've often thought that I'd like to own a cafe in some picturesque tourist resort. Not a large resort — just somewhere where I'd be sure of a steady stream of customers, different each day. I suppose it would make more sense to want regulars, but as it's only a daydream, I can indulge in my fancy for variety.

☐ I once thought about going into the lucrative business of repairing transistor radios. Take one to a shop and they'll want a fiver to have a look and tell you what may be wrong, and then there's the cost of repairing it.

Me and a friend had some time on our hands at work as we were on breakdown cover. We were electricians and someone always had a faulty radio to mend. We found out that very rarely was it a faulty component, but nearly always a dirty contact or a dry soldered joint. A few hours of touching this and pulling that usually produced a crackle which pointed to the fault. There was never any charge. Sometimes, very rarely in fact, if the radio was a good 'un, we'd tell the owner it was not repairable hoping he'd say, "Well throw it away then" which he often did and we'd keep it for ourselves.

☐ It was after my divorce that I made up my mind to be independent in spite of having three children to care for.

I considered what talents I had and decided that typing was the thing I could do best, and if I could take in work at home I could both earn a living and rear my children without them thinking they had been deserted by both parents.

My mum lent me the money for an electric typewriter. I could not go to the bank for a loan as I was not wage earning. I also bought a desk and chair from a friend whose husband had left her and she wanted rid of his things. I then converted half my bedroom into an office and was all set to embark on the great adventure of becoming self-employed. I put an advertisement in the local paper and that was how work started to come in.

After nearly five years I feel I have really achieved something in life. Last year I moved to a larger house and I have converted one of the two living rooms into an office. Far from being the useless person my ex-husband told me I was, I am now supporting my children. I paid back the loan to mum at so much a week, invested in a word processor out of my earnings and I have restored my self-esteem.

☐ My daughter's third birthday prompted me into becoming self-employed. I had ordered her cake and was so excited at its arrival, but when we saw it, it was horrendously decorated in gaudy, glaring colours. There and then I decided to enrol at day and evening classes and I am now a fully qualified cake designer.

I used to work from home, but since last August I have rented premises in the Dark Arches in Leeds. Being my own boss has given me a new found freedom and my business is thriving. At times it gets lonely being by myself all day, but the creativity involved demands this solitude so it's roundabouts and swings really. It's a seven days a week profession but very satisfying to know that I am putting my skills to good use.

A few years ago I sold second hand baby clothes at a local market and managed a good turnover until the slump came. I suppose I could have sold cakes there too but it's difficult to sell iced cakes in the open

Stephen McClarence

air, so I decided to go for the Leeds premises once I saw they were empty. My husband says he feels proud of my success but at the same time I think he would like me to be just-a-housewife. I know I can never go back to being at home doing chores and looking after kids. My time now is for myself and I must move on and upwards.

☐ I've never tried to do any social climbing with the money I've made; it doesn't interest me. I still drink with the lads I drank with when I was at the pit. Sometimes I get lads I was at school with who were at the top of the class when I was nearer the bottom, wondering how I've done so well. I think the answer is I enjoy making money. It doesn't matter if at the end of the day I've made fifty or five hundred pounds, I'm happy if I've made something. And I've always enjoyed it, right from being a kid. I used to charge people a penny a time for a go on my bike and I kept my own hens and sold eggs when I was ten. I see nothing wrong with it. As long as I'm satisfied I'm giving a fair deal and my customer is happy with the price then it's alright by me. Of course I've been able to enjoy a lot more luxuries than if I'd stayed in the pit and so has my wife. She likes to collect Royal Doulton figures and we've had some good holidays, but I like to give a bit out locally as well. I sponsor Streethouse Rugby. I'd sooner do that than go to the ballet because it's something I understand. I also like to give a bit to charity, but you don't want thanking for that. The other day I had a letter from the hospital asking for a donation, some doctor or other was having his head shaved, so I sent them something. And the Salvation Army, I always give to them because they do good work and besides that, my mother was one.

☐ Before we began to be business women we went to Whiteley's Food Hall in Knightsbridge, London to survey and take note of what food is popular. We have no dish-washing facilities so all our plates are disposable, but we put ecology to the forefront when we buy in things. Sunday is our busiest day and all staff are present. We double the Monday to Friday ratio of takings on Sunday. We have a well stocked varied display of vegetarian foods alongside some conventional dishes alongside naughty-but-nice cakes.

I think we did well in the planning of our business. It took only six weeks from day one to the day we started.

☐ I've had to learn self-motivation and how to plan my time. Previously I've always worked for other people and they've done this planning for me. I write myself daily lists of jobs to be done and cross them off as I go along.

☐ A knitting machine isn't all fun, but if you are going to make money with one, then you cannot rely on two needles forever. Then the problems start. Dust was one I had

Kevin Reynolds

Stephen McClarence

to contend with. Every time the carriage went across, small fibres would be thrown up and go into my eyes, nose and throat. I had, if you like, a health and safety at work problem.

Jack solved it by bringing home one of those masks which paint sprayers use and fitted me up with a set of goggles. Thus attired I could sit all day and make pullovers, babies' jumpers and a whole array of knitted goods. Once when I was in full swing, the door bell went. Without thinking I went to the door and found the gasman. He looked surprised, I looked as if I had just landed. "Oh, I'm sorry" I said, "I was knitting."

☐ Friends and relatives all rallied round when I first began to design cakes and I needed their support. Though I feel sometimes that they put a price on the person they know, rather than on the time and effort that goes into producing a decorative cake, I have come to accept that as one of the irritations of the job.

Kick start

☐ My dad tried to start up a small business just after the war. He had been trained as a poster writer, but had become a factory labourer in 1940 when he was required to go into essential war work.

The soldiers were coming home and almost everyone required a poster for their front window or half light which said "Welcome Home Jim" or whatever. I think that he charged half a crown a time. A ridiculous price when you think of it and bearing no relationship whatever to his real costs. Mind, he always sold his labour cheap.

We lived in one downstairs room and after tea the living room table became his work bench. The tools of his trade were simple ones; turps, art paper, sable brushes and a straight edge. We lived a bit better in 1946 because of that on-the-side work. What I mean by that is that we ate bubble and squeak less frequently.

In the end the work had to stop. Up the road there was an official poster writer, an established firm, and its owner was in the Freemasons with our landlord. One day the rent collector reported that poster writing would have to stop because this wasn't business premises. If Dad persisted then he would have to move on. With two small children in the midst of a housing crisis, he hadn't really much choice.

☐ Demobbed after the 1939-45 war Dad started his own business as a jobbing builder. At first he transported his tools and materials on the carrier of a push bike he used for getting around but after he bought a canvas topped van with an open back that we sometimes used on Sundays for family outings to the coast.

Before the war he had served his apprenticeship as a plumber and had worked for the council and on new housing developments in the south. He had earned a reputation for 'eating work' which did not go down too well with his work mates on the council. It was somehow a foregone conclusion that Dad, with his capacity for work, should be eventually working for himself and not for others.

His business developed and he set on more men. At one time he employed about six, but work in the building trade was prone to booms and slumps. Gradually the slumps became more frequent. Then there was always also the business of waiting for payment. People seldom paid straight away once the work had been finished.

In the end Dad spent more and more of his time looking for work to keep the men employed, gradually getting in debt to pay wages to a workforce he was reluctant to finish. Eventually his health broke down, he lost his business and the comfortable home he had worked hard to provide for his family. He recovered later and worked for others, but outside the village, coming home only at weekends.

☐ I was invalided out of the RAF and took the opportunity to go into partnership in this video shop as an offshoot from my father's mobile video libraries. He gave me a lot of help and advice as did a number of on-going video businesses. I was very apprehensive about putting all my life savings into the business. We were going in totally blind, but after doing our homework we decided it was a lucrative investment.

Being your own boss gives you the advantage of not being told what to do by anybody, and you feel more or less in control of your life. You can do what you want when you want, but if you take advantage of that too much, your business does not go anywhere. As a reward for taking the plunge, as it were, I am watching our business grow and prosper.

The winter is our best time because during the summer people do not bother with videos. The World Cup has also affected our sales lately. Our only real setback was when our distributor and wholesaler, Video House, closed down without warning. Now we have overcome that. We are dealing direct with video companies.

☐ A young bloke in Featherstone set up a barber's shop above an electronics place, he called it "Upper Cut". Well, I suppose he would, wouldn't he? The story went round that he made customers welcome by asking

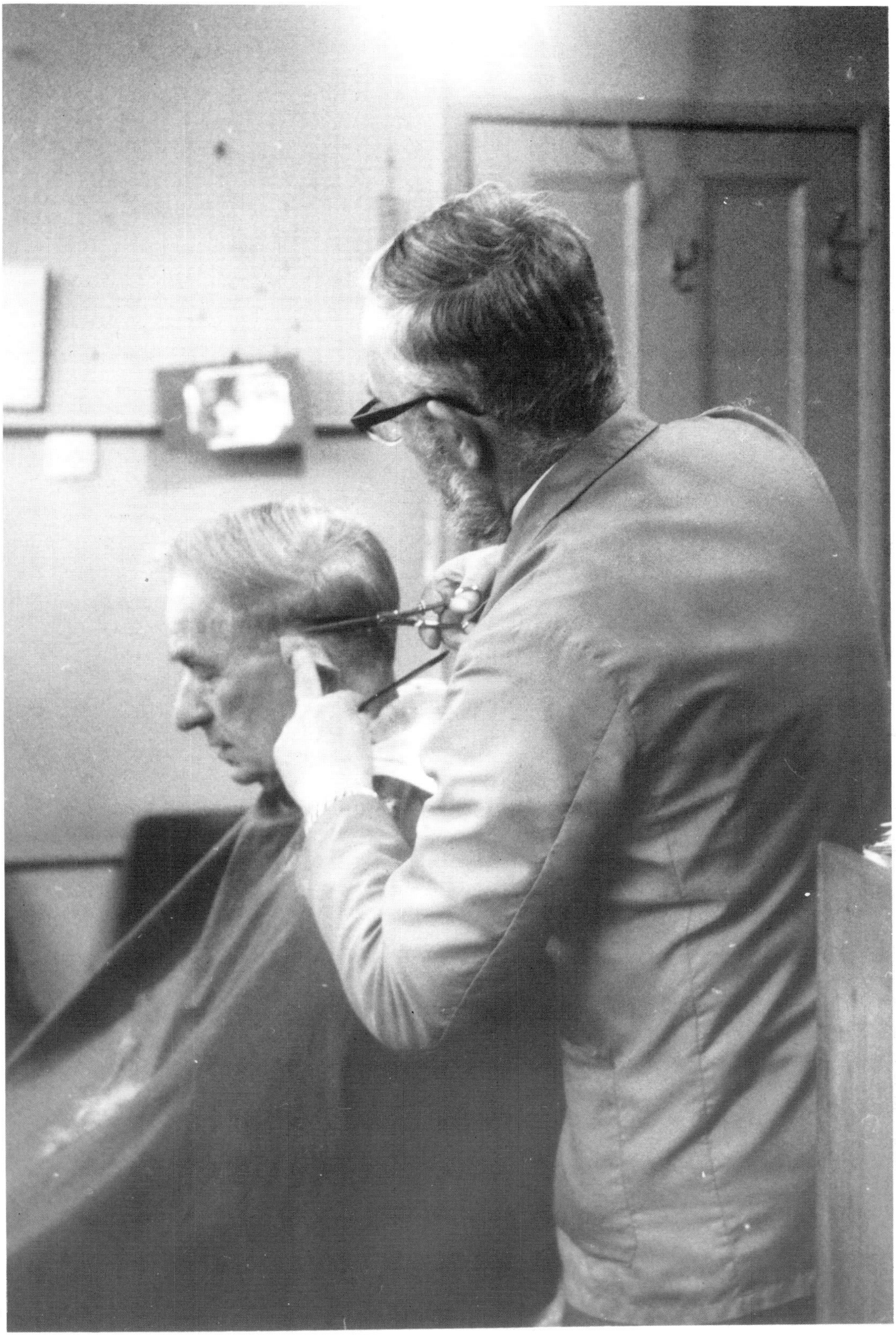

Stephen McClarence

them, "Is it the usual today sir?" If anybody came back with "It's the first time I've been in" he'd say, "I mean my usual, sir, not yours."

Another story involved a rather belligerent ex coal miner sat in the chair. The barber got to the end of his cutting and asked "Would you like anything on it?"
"Aye," said the miner, "a bloody balaclava."

☐ Making stained glass lamps and windows started as a hobby which I learned from books. Then, going round pubs I noticed that everywhere seemed to be ripping out windows and replacing them with stained glass. That gave me the idea that there was a market. Two of us set up together and, to be honest, we expected instant success. We'd sold to friends and on market stalls, but we had no business experience and no real ideas about marketing and book-keeping. We've been learning on our feet but even now the money we make wouldn't finance a full time worker. Me and my mate make all the stuff, store it in garages and lofts and our wives run the shop for free. We couldn't survive if we didn't have other jobs as well, but survival isn't the only reason I do it. In my other job I feel bored and frustrated but after a day making a lamp or a window I can say to myself, "I've done something worthwhile today."

The Enterprise

☐ When the boat was working for thirty years out of Tenby, taking trippers to Caldey Island, it was called *The Enterprise,* so we kept the name and added the slogan "The Enterprise boldly going where no boat has gone before." Very true — we travel down the River Aire from Ferrybridge to beyond Knottingley chemical works. On the surface it is an unspectacular journey, but if you're looking for education there's little better. It's a grand trip. I talk about the sights on the outward journey, and on the way back, sing to a tape. There's a bar and food.

☐ We spent a lot of time choosing the right unit. A good location is very important. We liked this one because it has just the one window. We can make an interesting display and tempt people in to look at what else we've got. Some of the other units are like goldfish bowls; people can see everything you've got without coming through the door. Also it's a good strategic location near the food, everybody is interested in food.

☐ I've learned a lot in the last two years about dealing with people. I used to be personally quite shy and one of the hardest things about setting up in business was learning to talk to people.

Some customers amuse me though. The other week a bloke came in to order a stained glass window. It was to be 36" x 11" and in this space he wanted the name of his house with a ballet dancer at the left side, a wind surfer in the middle and at the right a black cat. He was completely serious and had gone to all the trouble of cutting out pictures from magazines to show me what the ballet dancer and wind surfer were to look like. I couldn't possibly laugh, so I put the instructions on the order shelf, looked him in the eye and said "I'll get back to you."

Window shoppers also forget that you're inside and that you can hear everything they say. As well as stained glass windows we make lamps and terrariums. One day two women stopped outside the shop.
"What's that?" one of them asked pointing at a large terrarium.
"A terracotta," the other woman announced, "fancy you not knowing that, I thought everybody knew they were terracottas."

☐ You sometimes get into business accidentally. I got the tools of my trade in an unusual way.

My father was a bus driver who went to the barber's about once a month for a trim. The barber upset him with all his scandal about bus drivers and conductresses "having it off" so he walked out in disgust and never went back. It's funny therefore that I should become a barber. My introduction went like this.

Kevin Reynolds

I would be about thirteen years of age and I had a marvellous mouth organ with a double octave key. I was walking past the Theatre Royal in Albion Street when a well dressed man came out of the theatre. "Can I have a look at your mouth organ son?" he asked. I gave it to him. He played it like an expert and then said he needed it for his act, he took me back to his theatrical digs near the railway station. A lot of theatre acts in those days stayed in a boarding house in Castleford called Mizpah House. He showed me to his wife and then offered me fifteen shillings in cash and two pair of hair clippers. I said I would ask my dad. Well, Dad was delighted and I made the swap.

That's what set me on trimming hair.

Tentative steps

☐ If you work at the Centre for the Unemployed you meet a large number of people who have lost their jobs for a whole variety of reasons, but in recent years, mainly through redundancy or ill health.

About four years ago, Radio One ran a two day weekend phone-in where listeners were encouraged to ring in to a local number and seek the advice of 'experts' on any aspect of welfare rights and employment.

Staff from the Centre for the Unemployed were asked to join the team of local 'experts' in a large room, owned by MSC in Leeds. That week I found myself spending two days sitting at a telephone with my head-phones on, listening and responding to people's problems. The calls came from all over the country.

☐ Everyone has that little knick-knack gathering dust that they acquired in a moment of weakness, the dreaded 'bargain'. Collecting rubbish must be one of my major pastimes, but maybe one in which I am not on my own. Having a clear-out or jumble sale is one way in which to get rid of junk, but my major reason for involvement in a car boot sale was to earn some extra cash. It was to be held at Sandwell Middle School for some charity or other, advertised with home-made posters. Helen, my friend, boasted the fact that she was an experienced junk seller and so I put myself in her hands. Easy, I thought, we arrive with a boot full of bits and bobs and people will buy, but I was not optimistic of the final result. I sorted out a pile of what I classed as rubbish and one of interest, books, old clothes. Then Helen sorted out what she thought was of interest, old make-up, pot dogs with pieces missing, butter dishes, odd mugs. Surely I thought, people wouldn't buy this lot — I was to find out shortly how wrong I could be.

As we approached Sandwell School the next day I was astounded by the number of vehicles parked outside. Helen's adventure was running, "Shut your eyes and windows and stay by me." She was sounding our battle campaign. My feelings were excitement mixed with pleasure. As we rounded the tarmac area we saw the stalls set out, with people gathering round. "Quick" said Helen and she leapt into action. Out with the borrowed pasting table and she was working with speed, setting out the stall. I stood like a blubbering jelly as bits of my old junk were thrust into my hands. Twenty pence, ten pence, I began getting excited by the pace and speed of the selling. Next minute I was haggling away.

Shortly a voice close to me shouted in my ear "How much for this love?" I looked. It was Helen's jacket. Sorry I was just about to say, "I'll give you a tenner" — "Done" shouts Helen, "I only bought it for a fiver off Wakey market," she whispered in my ear and we collapsed laughing.

The day soon quietened down but that selling fever had really caught me and I understood the phrase "sell your own grandmother" much more clearly.

☐ When I set up I didn't anticipate how tough I'd have to become. At first I was naive and didn't ask for deposits on pictures people ordered. Then I had to get used to insurance men, marketing men, pension men, all ringing me up, trying to sell me

BUNNY

their deals. I've also had to educate my family; they all thought I was doing better than I was, just because I had a shop. They didn't understand that all the money that came in was going straight back out again.

☐ As a young nurse I was always dreaming of finding cures for dreadful illnesses such as cancer and cystic fibrosis, diseases which greater people than I had failed to cure. I did however, discover a cure for Athlete's Foot which also prevented the disease. Not at all the romantic Madame Curie image I had built up for myself. My prototype involved the use of cotton wool, but this proved uncomfortable so I made use of toilet tissue which I formed into the shape of a knuckle duster which was inserted under the toes.

I decided to patent my invention, but first I had to find out how and where to apply. I got the required information from the local library and sent off my application to the Office of Patenting in London. It cost me ten pounds for a short term protection which applied to the UK only. The next move was to approach a pharmaceutical company. I chose Scholl who market so many products for foot care.

I sent diagrams and accompanying notes and to my surprise I had a reply from the company within a few days. Later a representative of the company visited me to discuss the product. We signed an agreement of secrecy which was witnessed by my secretary.

Some weeks later I received a letter saying that Scholl were not interested in prevention as it would affect their sales of Athlete's Foot treatment.

☐ When I worked at the pit as an electrician, a certain panel had a removable unit which, using the spanner that the firm provided, could take some minutes to remove. Your knuckles inevitably suffered. I sawed the end off the proper spanner and welded it to a cranked rod and I could remove the box in seconds. When I coyly suggested to someone that it might be worth something,

I was completely put off with stories from, "Anything you make or invent at the pit, belongs to the Coal Board" to "No, I don't think much to that idea". Before long every electrician at the pit had one, they knew how much better it was. I heard some years later that the firm came out with a similar tool. I didn't tell them about it.

☐ I started off by making shirts for Paul because he was singing in a rock band and liked to look a bit different. Then all his friends started asking for them too and I thought perhaps it was a way to earn some money by working for myself. I didn't like working for someone else because they don't respect your talent. At first I tried selling them on a casual basis in the market. We did quite well, with low overheads and a few days' trading, we made a good profit. But people don't spend big money in markets and we were trying to establish a unique product. Also, people like to try things on and it can be a bit cold stripping off in the open air. Moving into the unit at Dark Arches seemed the natural step up.

I sat opposite the woman who was responsible for providing information on "setting up your own business" and it soon became obvious that she just could not cope with all the enquiries which came flooding in to her. It seemed that every other phone call was from someone who was unemployed and had given up hope of finding new employment and so their enquiry was about setting up a business. The call was their last desperate bid to get themselves back into work.

They had no idea what type of business they wanted to start or how they would finance it, but they had no other hope and were clutching at the last straw.

I don't know how many people ever took the first tentative step beyond that phone call. We will never know how many people actually tried starting their own business. The only thing we can be certain of is that only a very small number of enquiries proved successful or we would have so many small firms operating that the unemployment problem would be solved.

☐ If you want to set up a new business, try to get one which is to do with being born, being wed or dying. They never go out of fashion. Well, leastways two of them don't.

☐ For me anything goes in business. I typeset what's given me. If it's racist or soft porn, that doesn't bother me. I'm offering a service and it's not my job to safeguard morals. I would draw a line at paedophilia but little else. Sometimes I'm worried. A Militant teacher wanted something done for a pamphlet. I didn't like doing it, but in the end I did.

On the other hand Julie wouldn't touch pornography in any form, but she wouldn't mind political things. You have to remember business is business.

☐ We've seen a lot of people thinking about business who fall into a variety of categories. There is the man who cannot become a businessman however hard he tries. He asks for information and then does nothing. Then there are the ones who go off like a rocket and are quickly successful. Unless they come back and tell you, then it is not clear how far they get. In the middle there is another group. If they're in that group, the person could make it or not. A lot depends on the way things work out.

☐ My daughter and son-in-law decided that they would use the redundancy money to set up for themselves. She had experience in the clothing industry, but he had worked in mining right up into his fifties, but it's never too late to learn. Jodhpurs were what they produced.

He took the £40 allowance and did what women know how to, but not many men; he unpicked a pair. Then with this pattern he started. Now he's an expert cutter and handles that side of the business.

What threatens them are the rates. No one knows what this poll tax will bring. When they went into the Featherstone Enterprise Zone on that Coal Board Scheme, they thought they knew where they stood, but after the area was sold from under them, things are not so clear. Yet for all that, they are employing ten workers and gaining a reputation.

For instance, Streethouse bought a strip for one of the local teams, then in a key match they discovered that the team they were playing had the same colours. They turned out a new strip within the week. You couldn't get that service from Korea.

☐ When I started up in business just after the war, we had no running water and no electricity, everything was hand operated. One farmer came in with a length of iron bar, he wanted a dozen ½″ holes drilling in it. I said I couldn't do it just then, but if he wanted to do it himself, he could use the big hand drill. He started off full of enthusiasm. The next time I looked, he changed from right to left hand, then both hands. Finally I saw him leaning right over the drill — and he'd only done two holes!

There was one customer I never liked, always full of his own importance. One day he called and left a repair saying "I'll pick it up on my way back."
"Aye, you can pick it up on your way back," I said, and then, just as he got to the door, I shouted after him "but it'll not be ready." He had to come back then and make a proper arrangement.

Well, do I declare?

☐ People get sucked into the black economy without realising it, or even knowing what the black economy is.

They are claiming benefits and live from one week to the next without sufficient money to meet the costs of their everyday living.

Then one day they may get the chance to earn a few extra pounds doing a bit of casual

Stephen McClarence

work. This could be anything from building a wall for a neighbour, knitting a jumper for a friend of a friend, helping out the local window cleaner for a few days or doing a bit of van driving for a firm.

How many people are going to think about needing to declare this work to the benefits office and the tax man? Of the ones who do think about it, how many are going to decide not to bother as it is such a small job which will only last a day or two?

Believe it or not, there are actually quite a lot of people who, being totally honest, upstanding citizens, decide they must declare the work to the benefits office. That's when their problems can begin. They might expect that they will not be paid benefits for the days they have worked. They might expect that their benefits will be reduced by the amount they have earned, except for £5. But what they don't expect is that the benefits giro, upon which they rely so heavily, may be delayed for days or even weeks, whilst benefit officers ask them to fill in additional forms, re-examine their entitlement to benefits and generally cause a lot of extra hassle. Having to answer questions and fill in additional forms is bad enough, but the main problem is what do they live on until the giro comes? You can bet they haven't any savings left in the bank if they've been living on benefits for a while!

So what happens if another chance comes along for this person to earn a few extra pounds. Some may think "I was just unlucky last time" and dutifully declare the work again. Others will think, "not likely, I'm not risking all that hassle again for just a few hours' work and not much money at the end of it" and so they either refuse the job, or more likely, decide to take the work and just keep quiet about it. Well, can you blame them?

My own boss and very grand

☐ I shivered and shook on the windswept field as I pitched my paste board table, then onto it teemed every bit of junk I'd amassed or had been given for my very first car boot sale. My purse strings had of late become tight and I was desperate to earn a little bit extra behind the taxman's back, so wrapped up in my thickest sweater and with ample supplies of tea and sarnies, I set to work on my first foray into the commercial world.

This new venture rather excited me as I had myself always been a bit of a rummager and believed I knew what appealed to people of the same mind. So I confidently displayed my wares, and I gave the full treatment to each and every one who idly strolled up to my trestle table. I felt the adrenalin begin to flow as I struck my first deal of the day.

I hadn't chosen a tin to store my cash for it gave me utter joy to feel extra cash run through my fingers into my pocket. I began with a small float of about two pounds in copper. It proved to be a wise move for to be short of change meant a lost sale and as it was my first attempt I didn't want even one disappointment.

I was surprised at how quickly my new venture had got off the ground. I only mentioned it in passing to one or two of my friends but soon my drive was filled with black plastic sacks of cast-offs, bric-a-brac, shoes and books. You name it, I had it. Family too all pitched in their bit and I had a great time ferreting out all the best sellers and chucking out the real rubbish as it became obvious that if you asked for free junk, that was what you got.

At first my family did a bit of smirking and I acquired all the usual nick-names. "Second hand Rose" seemed to be the favourite. Things were going so successfully that I breezed along thinking they'll laugh on the other side when I make my big pile of readies. I felt very grand having the nerve to stand in all weathers and see people who knew me well failing to recognise me. They had seen me the night before in some hostelry, done up to the nines, and now they saw me dressed like a tinker and glad of a few extra bob.

My decision to try this new lark was not thought out carelessly. I knew I had the knack of dealing with people and setting up conversations with anyone always gave me satisfaction. To deal with the public on a profit making basis did not cause me any intrepidation whatsoever as I knew I could be very persuasive if the need arose. So I felt no qualms at becoming a carbooter.

Every week that I pitched my table, be it in a school yard, field or hall, I felt the tremor of expectancy and enthusiasm of making a few quid to tide me over for another week. Morning, of course, was always the high point of the day, but after a few hours of wheeling and dealing, I began to feel a bit jaded. Indeed it is exhausting work having to be affable all the time especially when the public are trying their best to have your wares for nothing. They think in terms of profit and don't take into account my stall fee and how many hours I have stood there praying for customers.

After a few weeks I felt I had been at this game for years and I was soon able to sort out the genuine bargain hunters from the market dealers. Dealers came along with mammoth sized shopping bags whilst the ordinary folk made do with carrier bags, so it wasn't long before I began to add a copper or two on to the wise guys of the rag trade. I even went as far as to hide the good stuff to give the others a chance.

Before long what I was doing became public knowledge and my acquaintances on the estate assumed I was making vast sums on the side. Many times I was quizzed as to what I could knock out on a Sunday but my lips were firmly sealed. I wouldn't talk therefore it was deemed that I was getting above my station.

I persevered and soon my mind was putting into action a plan to rent a market stall. My few months working a car boot sale had given me valuable experience of the public and of their fickle ways. From experience came the conclusion that I would be better off having a permanent place of trading so with my new idea bandied back and forth, I booked my name in at the Market Office.

Being my own boss seemed very grand and I never gave much thought to the fact that I had gone into business without any professional advice. I assumed my success was down to common sense and a good sense of timing. Of course it never entered my head that there would be swings and roundabouts. I never thought about the winter months, but gaily plodded on jingling the profits and feeling chuffed that I was doing something of my own. The only disadvantage of working for myself as I could see it, was that I had to keep a tight rein on the cash flow and keep myself stocked up with supplies. Most nights I retired to bed feeling pleasure that I had amassed some profit.

After a few months though I began to feel the pinch. There was a general slump. The market authorities were cutting deeply into our profits by increasing our stall rents and dictating the time when we could finish our business. They said 4 p.m. whereas we stall holders stressed that by 3 p.m. the market swiftly emptied as people headed home. I had taken on this new project instinctively believing it would lead me to other more lucrative marketing, but it soon became apparent I would not be able to uphold repeated increases in rents. The falling off of trade meant that my initial capital was not secure. The control I had over what I could and could not do was not absolute. I was not my own boss but subject to seasonal fluctuations. On the other hand I had no one to answer to if I chose to shut up shop. Being a one woman band did help, I was only responsible for myself. I knew I could never afford to pay anyone to help me for I was selling only in a small market, so if I went bust only I suffered.

Stephen McClarence

There's no business like no business
There's no business I know

THERE'S NO BUSINESS LIKE NO BUSINESS

Succeeding or Failing

Good stools have four legs

☐ I'd hate to run a business on my own because I can't imagine having all the skills you need, from developing new ideas to working out the finances. I see business like trying to sit on a stool. If the stool has one leg, it's going to fall over; if it has two, you'll always be trying to balance and if it has three, you're steady but you can still fall over. There are four of us in our business which means we're rock solid but can also cope if one person is ill.

☐ Some are born with skills. I know one who started off moving office furniture with one small van. After he had done it for a bit he recognized that he ought to be into retailing as well as delivering. From haulage he moved into buying and selling and eventually into design. Nothing elaborate there. Just the ability to see a gap in the market and know how to fill it. People like him make it upwards without having very much appreciation of what they are doing. It's all experience. They know how to read a balance sheet. They also have a high appreciation of self-worth. They believe in themselves. The desire to enter business is very rarely born of desperation.

The woman of a family sometimes follows in with the man but not always. In almost all cases there has to be a partner who is the bread winner. Small firms don't generate enough money straight away, so there has to be something to live on in the period between the invoices going out and the cash coming in.

Another type of business has a woman who produces a base income. She protects the brood while he tries to get the business off the ground. To help out she starts to get financial skills. She becomes the book-keeper. She may already have the basic secretarial skills or have been involved in a small business before. In the early stages she writes up the accounts. If she's innovative then she transfers them to the computer. As the business expands she is replaced by someone full-time. She doesn't resent this. She goes back to jobs within the family. Occasionally some go full time.

☐ Sometimes whole family units get involved. There is a firm at Langthwaite Grange which started that way. Initially there were two husbands and wives. One man saw a niche in repackaging glass. He and his wife would buy in the glass and make a decision as to whether the flaws in it were so bad they had to remelt, or whether the quality was of a tolerable level. Remember they might have been dealing with perfume at £100 an ounce so they couldn't afford flaws in the glass. They employed local female labour to sort manually — whisky bottles, coffee jars, scent bottles — they would look at them, sort and repackage. It's a skilled job.

Four years ago they started with four women and now employ fifty people. Local labour coming as it does from the sewing trade, posesses a high level of manual dexterity. Women from one trade easily transfer to another. They saw that and capitalised on it.

☐ Don't employ staff unless you absolutely have to; that's when your troubles begin. Go into a partnership if you must or employ the family but do not take on strangers. They'll never be as committed as you. Why should they be? In the long run they've nothing to keep them with you and many

will move on for a pound or so in their wage packets.

☐ My first company was a pasta factory in Malta which was influenced by God, or so the workforce thought. I had been there for just long enough for the workforce to approach me. "Could a priest come in and take confession?" a woman representative asked. Since I couldn't see how it would affect production I agreed. On a selected day a priest turned up with what looked like a suitcase. It wasn't, it was a portable confessional. He assembled it and sat inside.

After all was over the spokeswoman came up again. "Would I like the Father to bless the machines?" Nothing ventured nothing gained. I let him and he went round with holy water and a brush, sprinkling holy water. I was impressed but more impressed when we had no breakdowns for four months.

☐ The local economy has been dominated by large employers in traditional industries in the past, mainly British Coal. In the Economic Development Department we now see the need to help the local economy to diversify and grow. Some growth can come in the form of major inward investment like the Japanese firm Pioneer, but some diversification and graft should also come from within, from the creation and development of vibrant small industries involved in diverse sectors and trade, from tourism to engineering.

☐ We have a very small small firms assistance scheme called Workline that has two prongs to it. One is to help local firms to employ and train young unemployed people. The training is the most important part. The other is to assist firms to buy equipment so that they can create jobs. The scheme is targeted as much as possible to ensure that young unemployed people obtain transferable skills. We also target the assistance to firms both geographically, for

instance, to the coalfield areas, and to people setting up in types of business that find it difficult to get financing from private sources. These include co-operatives, women and redundant miners although, of course, we help other types of business too. By showing our confidence in such a variety we help them get funding from other sources. A small amount of council funding levers out considerable amounts from other public agencies and the private sector.

Co-ops aren't grocers

☐ I'd describe a co-op structure as being a bit like a box of chocolates, with lots of different shapes. You need people to fill the different shapes. If you end up with a square that's supposed to fit a round hole, you've got problems.

☐ We started with a product and the philosophy developed later. It doesn't take a genius to see that there's a gap in the market and the north is lagging a bit behind the south where vegetarianism and things like that are concerned. Wakefield needs a good vegetarian restaurant.

The times are on our side. Concern about additives and mad cow disease means that a lot of people do not wish to go to old style eating places and are ready for a change. We reckon that we can provide it. We have something unique to offer and if we fulfil ourselves in the process, so much the better.

Of course we benefit because there are a lot of advantages in being in a co-operative. We can control our work environment and be directly involved in decision making processes. The nine-to-five job is a complete straitjacket; there's no adventure, no risk. It's the type of life style which completely pisses me off. Co-operatives, by contrast, feel right.

☐ It's words really. You can't go into South Elmsall and tell people to form co-operatives. The Co-op is a grocer's. No more can you put over the council shops words like enterprise. Say enterprise round here and what comes into your mind: "private enterprise." Well people don't want that. You've got to get the words right. Mind, I'm only a caretaker.

☐ The Co-ops officer from our area — not Leeds, not Wakefield — called a meeting of the groups working as Co-ops in our area. What a collection. There was an advertising agency who in all the two hours we were there didn't mention their name, a performance group who did not perform in public and us.

☐ We work in a co-operative way but are not technically a co-op. Our key workers all get the same salary, but we have a management committee on which other people sit. Not a lot of time is taken up in discussion to which everyone comes, but we do have sub groups which discuss specific matters. These meet on a regular basis. One of our key workers has taken up the task of drawing up an agenda. I don't think that any of us could cope with an organisation in which an inordinate length of time was spent talking, talking, talking.

After ten years of successful practice, I cannot remember anyone sitting round discussing if we have a co-operative structure or not, although it must have come up when we discussed our constitution and chose to be a limited liability company.

☐ People say that you can't be a socialist and a business man. That's nonsense. A lot of businesses start off from when a person says I'm fed up being exploited by someone else. I'll find a product which I believe in, produce it and then market it for the benefit of others. A local history publishing house in the fifties was transformed by a Newcastle publisher who was a Marxist. The revolution in tourist publishing also started from that firm.

Then there is Suma, the wholefood co-operative in Leeds. That started when a few friends took to bringing health foods back from London in sacks, packaging them in a house and selling them door to door around Leeds. They were a co-operative with commitment to an idea; the idea that people could and should eat healthier food. Ten years later the world caught up with Suma.

That's the other thing you notice about socialist businesses. Because, by and large, socialists are more intelligent than conservatives, they are often in advance of the market, freer thinkers. What you can't be is a socialist and financier at the same time.

☐ I was made redundant in the early 80s from a large tractor manufacturing company. Six hundred of us were given notice on the same day, "Finish at the end of that week." It struck me at the time that since cuts were made across all departments; sales, design and production, pooling of such expertise plus redundancy money could have allowed us all to form our own tractor manufacturing plant. Ironically if I had tried a few months earlier to interest 599 colleagues they would all have said "No, I already have a steady job" or "Good idea, but I have no money available". Now that everyone had no job and enough cash available to consider the option, the market had almost collapsed. Now if I asked, everyone would have said, "Good idea but the timing is wrong".

Some days are diamonds

☐ I am part of a small community of four adults who live as a family and work together as a co-operative business. When we set up we had between us degrees in Biology, Biochemistry, History and Film, but we soon realised that this wasn't actually going to provide us with any work. All four of us are interested in role play — dragons, dungeons and vikings. Ian is a jobber and can make things, so when one of our friends asked us for a sword, he showed basic business acumen and asked "How much would you pay for it?"

We made this man a five foot sword. He

Stephen McClarence

showed it around and then all his friends wanted swords as well. We got together £1000 and set off thinking there was probably the potential to feed a couple of us if we were lucky.

We called ourselves 'Hoards of Albion', slightly tongue-in-cheek. We'd thought of calling ourselves 'Old Rope Enterprises' but thought the bank manager wouldn't take us seriously. Our market was re-enactment societies like the Sealed Knot. We were supplying them with weapons but discovered they wanted other things like water jugs and jewellery.

We had all sorts of people ringing us up for swords. One American lady wanted a really elaborate sword delivering to her fiance. He worked at a US airbase and we had this vision of ourselves turning up at the gates as arms dealers handing over the sword.

We soon found that more people buy jewellery than swords. With jewellery, most people make in the winter to sell in the summer at open air events. Our problem was we started in the spring. To get round the problem of having no stock we got hold of some gem stones. The first day we went out we packed our complete stock in a shoe box. Our sales for the day were £4 and just covered the petrol.

Whichever way you look at it, from now on although we have some freedom of choice, we are answerable for each other's cock-ups.

☐ I hate Thatcherism and all it stands for, but this much I will admit, five years ago, I could not imagine myself thinking of the problems of working in a small business. Now I think of them all the time. It's the problem solving I enjoy.

☐ We went to a craft fair recently selling our jewellery. Next to us there was a 19 year old lad sounding off to his mates.
"Look it's like this. You can get a stable job and have lots of money and be miserable.

On the other hand you could be like this lot, do what you like, have no money and be happy. Then again you could be like most of us, moderately well off and moderately miserable".

☐ Like many people I had the ambition to own my own business without any real idea of what to try. It was decided for me when, on leaving school, I went into a furnishing store as a salesman. I stuck it out but the wish to be my own boss was always with me, and the wish came to a head about the time of the miners' strike in 1984.

Things had been pretty slack for some months and the poor pay was further reduced when lack of sales made for less commission. The final nail in the coffin was hammered home with the news of a four day week. I decided that it was now or never. With financial help from family and friends, two silent partners and a furniture upholsterer who would share the premises, I opened up a furniture store.

I reasoned that if I could succeed in a mining village during a national strike, I would survive. My first big cash outlay and risk was to buy in my first stock of furniture and beds. I now had to plan my selling strategy and I drew on my previous experience and some never to be forgotten advice from my former boss, "Give people a service and you'll win hands down."

This is what I did. Nothing was too much trouble for the customer. I opened the shop six days a week and stayed open late until 9 pm on Tuesdays, and I was always willing to open up at anytime to suit a customer's needs. This entailed sometimes coming in on Sunday or late at night. I also set up an efficient after-sales service which has paid off manyfold.

The highest point in my venture was during 1986 when many miners were given redundancy. Furniture and beds were one of the main things that they spent their money on. I was very grateful for that.

☐ I got a phone call this morning from someone in Liverpool wanting to set up as a publishing house and bookshop. "I've been told it would be useful to talk to you," she said "Oh, yes" I said a bit cautiously, "what would you like to know?"
"Well, how did you, like, do it?"
I took a deep breath! How to compress ten years of energy, agony and daily grind into a sentence?

They'd got the promise of £60,000 from Liverpool City Council. Our first grant was £150. They wanted to publish books by people who wouldn't ordinarily get into print. "Fine, how are you going to sell them?" I asked, "In the bookshops," she said.

She had no knowledge of the retail book trade, no idea of marketing, no thought who the customers were. The concept of a bookshop was a room with books in. Where do you start?

☐ My dad's friend, Charlie, worked for a large company who made garden sheds. Eventually it made him redundant. Charlie has two girls and a wife, so it was important for him to use his redundancy money wisely. Charlie had a reputation for being a bit 'tight' with his money.

He bought an old warehouse/shed in the Ossett area and decided to set up a business doing what he knew best — making sheds and garden fences. He also let some of the space he did not use to other small companies in the same boat as himself. This turned out to be a very good idea.

He once told my dad that he could live off the income from his premises alone, although he still makes sheds. He enjoys it.

Charlie's success is not just due to him and his idea. The whole family went through a traumatic time in the early stages of his venture. His wife gave up her job to run the administrative side of the business because it was as desperately important to her as to him. In many ways, working as a team at work as well as at home, brought them closer and made the first few months of the venture easier. They could work out any problems as they both had the whole picture.

☐ Some customers are so innocent. This man from Selby market came wanting a poster. I didn't notice what his note said until I was at the word processor and then I almost fell off my stool. It read N.O.B. Cleaning Services.

☐ After working 35 years in the pit, the time came when I could hang my helmet up. The 12 month long miners' strike had been a traumatic experience both for me and my family. When the strike was over, the atmosphere at the pit changed dramatically — morale was way down and even more so when it was decided that the pit had to close. I was just old enough to take redundancy and accept my pension; this I decided to do.

Failure and survival

☐ I took early retirement and wanted something to do. I needed to occupy my mind and thought running a little shop would be ideal; it would be a hobby especially during the winter months. We were too old for any other job and we wanted an inside job and regular hours so we came in blindly. We sunk a lot into that project but it didn't work out. It was the milkman who kind of persuaded us. He had the lease and it sounded good but when we asked to see the books he couldn't produce them. The timetable was all wrong, we were rushed you see. We had practically sold our bungalow and the people who were to buy it had been gazumped several times, so we gave our word that we wouldn't let them down. We landed ourselves with that promise.

We didn't have any help in getting started. The solicitor had his doubts about the whole thing but we were too far along the road to turn back. We had doubts but still we were excited at the idea of running a village shop. Neither of us had any experience of shop work, or business for that matter. What a way to go on.

We didn't expect to make a lot of money but we did think the shop would pay the rent, lighting and phone bills. That has proved to be totally wrong. We don't take enough to cover any of the bills. Villagers only come in for things they forget to get at the supermarket.

If anybody asked my advice about doing the same thing, I'd give them my honest opinion and say "Don't do it." We wouldn't like to see anyone else walk into the same situation. I'll tell you this, there is no need for a village shop in most villages.

We love living here but to survive, we both had to take casual work on. I do a bit of farm work and my wife does cleaning jobs. That's because we have to pay the bills somehow. We would like to give the shop up but we don't want to leave the village: we feel we were meant to come to live here. We'll keep on doing odd jobs while ever we can; as long as I can drive.

We've taken a big risk coming here; we gave up our own home, risked all our capital. What can we still lose? We sell newspapers but that's only sixteen a day and you make very little on them. We're just a tuck shop really.

Our idea of making a good living would be if we could afford a holiday each year, pay the rent and other overheads. There's not much chance of that.

☐ I made the classic error and failed miserably. That is I tried to expand too quickly and took out an initial capital loan which could not be supported by sales. Eventually the work dried up and the promise of the first year's trading was not fulfilled in the second.

When the crunch came I had to recognise that there was no capital reserve to fall back on. If I had one bad month it would take two months to catch up. A medium size company with twenty workers might have been able to diversify and acommodate the drop in revenue. I was alone.

There's nothing more dispiriting than turning up in an office with four walls and knowing that the phone is unlikely to ring.

☐ The problem with most businesses is

Stephen McClarence

that they believe that you can get things right and stay on one track for ever. The truth is that few products have qualities which allow you to do that.

☐ The amateurism that exists in even middle sized business is unbelievable. I was once given the job of marketing a new wallpaper product. It was just the right time to hit the public and they had sufficient capital to invest in a good range of quality advertising. I told them before we started that they had got the strategy wrong but they were sure that when I had brought in the customers, using a variety of techniques of which a full page colour advert in the *Sunday Times* was the top end, then all would be well.

The requests for information came in post vans full. They couldn't cope. They had not got the product into their retail outlets. People were asking for hessian wall paper which could be manufactured but could not be purchased on the High Street.

☐ After twenty four years in the roller covering industry, I became completely disillusioned. The company to whom I had given those years of loyal service was in decline. I had progressed from sales representative to Regional Manager and subsequently became the Sales Manager for the roller division.

For some months I had been 'head hunted' by a much bigger company who were also one of our competitors. I made the move just before the company closed down its roller division. My old colleagues were unfortunately made redundant. It was at that point that three of the men approached me for financial backing to set up in business. We had discussed the possibility of buying from our ex-employers. I agreed to put up some of the finance and that is how the company was launched. Our aim was to produce a better market product than the existing industries; there was a gap in the market and we felt sure that we could fill that gap.

The philosophy of the new partnership was to provide a service to local industries by putting factories where the customers were. In this way we could offer a quick and efficient service, therefore we required factory space, machinery and raw materials. My three partners had been my subordinates in the past but we had a good relationship so we became equals. After all we were working towards a common goal. We wanted to be successful and prosperous. Each of our skills was drawn on. My particular skills were managerial and marketing. One partner had technical skills and the other two were experts in production.

I have learned a great deal about finance and accounting since becoming self-employed and would advise anyone wanting to set up in business to make sure the finance is in place before starting. This is most important, do not underestimate the budget for commissioning a new business. Our capital outlay was raised from personal funds and bank loans.

The advantage of being your own boss is the control you have of your own destiny, also the excitement and challenge is a cure for boredom. There are some disadvantages which hopefully will lessen as we progress. They are long working hours and the deep sense of responsibility for others — partners and employees and for wealth and job creation in areas of high unemployment.

Help, I need somebody

☐ To set up reception, fax machines, duplicating facilities, the whole bag of tricks, you need capital which you cannot possibly afford right off. That's why we have set up resources centres in Castleford and South Elmsall. It's a good model.

☐ It's not only councils who see the need for common service support systems. Over in Ossett a woman has set up her own service. Some of the companies on her land rent premises in a straightforward way, but others opt for a different model. They pay into a central pool which gives them the use of the Fax machine, reception and telephone services and photocopier. They also get the meetings rooms and a canteen. This has got to be a good idea. Local government, central government and the private sector can see its benefits. What is needed next is creches.

☐ We fund the Wakefield Enterprise Agency to offer advice to businesses, mainly start-ups through surgeries at our two Resource Centres in Castleford and South Elmsall. Managed workspace is available there, as is day to day advice. This is available to help firms through the difficult formative stages.

What we are looking for are businesses with great potential, with new markets and products and processes, but these are difficult to find. Many people want to use their skills to set up their own business. Of course there may be many people with the same idea who are already in business. We try to help people to gain new skills so they have more choice and can be competitive. We also try to make some small improvement to local employment conditions by our policies towards low wages and encouraging firms to accept visits from trade union officials.

We have a financial assistance scheme so that we can keep in touch with the small firms sector and see what is going on and give help where it would be effective by networking and bringing in other agencies or by offering our own assistance.

☐ A flea climbing up the leg of a white elephant intent on sex — that's what Enterprise Centres can become if you don't watch out. There's ambition but it isn't very realistic. On the other hand if you can quickly relate into the community and set up a few successful small businesses then the word gets around and you begin to thrive.

We've managed to get several operations going and although industrial efficiency isn't the whole story of what we do, for we believe that we have community responsibilities as well, we can show four years of

Stephen McClarence

systematic growth. When we started, South Elmsall was in the doldrums. The coal strike had finished, pits had closed and there wasn't much hope about. We built slowly but surely so that today the old school building contains a technical design and drawing unit, a company making sun beds, sheet metal workers, a freelance video production team, leather belt manufacturers and a dressmaker. In the past we've encouraged a nut-and-bolt business and an entertainment impresario. This is what used to be the local middle school. We've also a computer centre, a creche and a place where we show exhibitions. We've also published two local interest books.

☐ It is amazingly difficult to get the local people involved because this is still looked on as a school. Actually we're not a school anymore, we're an Enterprise Centre, we're not into teaching except what people want to learn. It's not that you've got to learn Maths, English and History and that kind of thing. You come to learn what you need to learn and that's what it's about.

☐ In the short space of three years our

method of financing has had to change in order to survive in a very competitive market which has been greatly affected by high interest rates. High interest rates have created a spiral of delayed payments, customers are taking longer and longer to pay. This has created a cash flow problem. Factoring has been our answer. Let someone else be responsible for debt collection on a percentage basis!

The company has grown and diversified during its existence, we have two production factories and now we are in the process of opening a third one to produce our own raw materials; rubber and rubber compounds. The latest venture offers greater independence, reduces overheads and will create revenue by selling off some spare capacity to other companies.

Our plans for the next five years are to consolidate our present business and to expand by opening two further factories at least; these will be sited in different locations but in the centre of the industrial heartland. When that happens I will feel that I have really made it. Mind, I don't think I will ever retire, instead I will take longer holidays and work shorter days.

☐ After a career with a multi-national company and globetrotting around solving problems, this chap established, with one or two colleagues, a small business making windows. Some fifteen years later, now aged 70, he is wishing to 'work less' but has no-one to leave the technical side of the business to. As the firm has built itself a high quality niche in the market, production standards are the backbone of the enterprise and because of this he feels responsible for the families of his employees. His problem is how to relax the reins knowing that standards will become lower.

☐ My ambition is just a simple one, to be able to live comfortably. Whether I have one shop or one hundred shops, it won't change me. I'll know I've made it when I can sit back and watch other people doing the work, but I think I'll only stop when they put the last nail in the lid of my coffin.

My advice to others setting up in

Stephen McClarence

business? Think deeply and seriously and seek advice. Walk before you start to run or you will bury yourself.

Just one long holiday

☐ There's a man in Featherstone who took his redundancy after the first strike who must have been on more holidays than Onassis. For the first couple of years, every time he heard somebody was going away to Portugal or Spain or Tenerife, he'd say, "Right, I'll make one in for that," even if he'd just come back. He must have been on holiday with every family in Featherstone. His money's run out now, but at least he enjoyed himself with it.

☐ For some people, redundancy is a godsend. If the definition is widened to include early retirement, many people in their late 40s or early 50s are starting second careers, but they have an advantage; a pension behind them and probably a 'golden handshake'. If they came from the public sector, there are other advantages, for example, the pension is often index-linked.

Another advantage of the public servant is that he/she can develop contacts over the years. This is particularly true if they are at a senior level. This will benefit them in their 'second career'. This might be in dealing with suppliers of goods and services, or it might be that they have identified weaknesses in that local authority, civil service department or health authority, that they can later exploit by offering to come in and solve the problem in a consulting capacity.

This activity should be regarded as similar to 'insider dealing' in the City. Where the line should be drawn is uncertain. One possible approach is to offer early retirement to senior staff, only if they agree to work outside their former territory for a number of years.

What I am saying is that there can be another side to redundancy other than the heartbreak and despair which affects the vast majority. Those with the advantage of a good education, training and long experience can use the process to rejuvenate their lives and careers. But their activities could be at the cost of fairness and equity if they take advantage of the trust previously placed in them by the public they formerly served.

Small is dangerous

☐ It's no use setting up in business and not knowing the community. Take what happened in one of the villages.

During the strike, the best known chippy in the area used to rumble the potatoes for the miners' canteen. Then half way through, it changed hands. When the lads went down the next day, the new owner made no bones about where he stood. "Get back to work you bastards," he said, "rumble your own bloody potatoes."

Two nights later his windows went in. No one organised anything, it was just that the word got around. He got out quickly, no one went there, to buy was associated with scabbing. From then on it never thrived, people had got out of the habit of going. Now it's boarded up.

☐ When he first got the pub it did very well. He put on bar meals and did the place up. I called in for a pint occasionally but went up to eat when I won a raffle — a meal for two in the restaurant. After the meal he got chattering.

"I can't explain it," he said, "up to three months ago everything was champion but now trade has dropped back to a trickle."

"Have you ever been in the mining industry?" I asked.

"No."

"What jobs have you done?"

"Well I was once a policeman, but that was twenty years ago."

"Have you told anyone?"

"Yes, one or two."

That was it. The worst thing you could be. Around here it's best to keep your mouth buttoned up.

☐ Small business men or women get trodden all over by the big boys. You start off hoping to be a millionaire by the time you are thirty and just a little way down the line you realise that you are being shat on by the big boys.

As the law stands at the present, you cannot charge interest on outstanding debts. What that means is that the big firms hold on month after month and never pay your bills. They ignore your requests and what at the start looked like a good job, becomes part of a nightmare. To them you are a little Joe Bloggs and they know that there is another Joe Bloggs waiting round the corner.

Someone tried to get a Bill through Parliament to help us, but the MPs talked it out.

☐ My biggest problem at the moment is that manufacturers are way behind with orders and whereas they would let me pick up goods in my own transport, they now insist on delivering themselves, arguing that I'm jumping the queue. Some firms have an eight weeks delivery time and this is difficult to explain to customers.

☐ For a small manufacturer in agriculture it was difficult because farmers would bring your own produce back for repair. They could not do that with a large manufacturer. What got me was that they would bring them straight out of the piggery, a whole trailer load of hoppers that had to be hosed down before I could repair them. I had to oblige them because I was dependent on them for new orders. Some repairs took almost as long as a new product, but I couldn't charge for the price of a new one. Economically, repairing for farmers was a disaster.

Sometimes, I would have to get out to do a repair in a field, perhaps a combine harvester had hit a tree root and buckled. I had to load my trailer up with all the gear I thought I might need, and then try to improvise a repair up on the hillside. Once

I remember using the combine's own hydraulic system to pull itself straight. That gave me great satisfaction. Farmers always expected that you could do it, they never thought anything was beyond repair.

Once a farmer asked me to go out, just before harvest and cut an eight foot binder down to six foot. I had to cut two foot off everything that operated the machine and get it to work again afterwards. The reason he wanted it done, was because the binder would not go through any of his gateways and the farmer thought it was easier for me to cut it down that for him to widen the gateways.

☐ "I want this, can you do it for me?" is something I get asked a lot. It's one of the things that gives me great satisfaction when I know I've provided somebody with something unique.

Suiting the customer can be a bit of a trap though. I went through a stage when people would look at my paintings and say, "They're a bit miserable aren't they, can't we have something more sunny?" I tried to oblige and started doing pictures with lambs in the corners. I hated doing it and the pictures didn't sell either. It taught me that the best thing to do is concentrate on painting a picture I like and worry about selling it later. In the end, people get round to liking your style.

All you ever talk about is business

☐ When we sold the Off Licence there was a bit of money left over so I gave him twelve months to make the business pay. I don't like risks and gambles. I like the money there, but this had to be different because of the cost of the word processor.

We are now in our second year. It's been a hard one. There have been no family outings and apart from a weekend in December, no breaks. This is profit year.

☐ Some people don't draw a distinction

Stephen McClarence

between having your own business and working from home. They should; working from home is dreadful.

Of course there are advantages. I work in the room at the back of my garage so I can leave the house when I want to, go to the lavatory and make a cup of coffee without anyone having the right to question what I am doing. But the disadvantage is that I am totally accessible. From nine o' clock in the morning until midnight they think they have a right to phone. The other night one man phoned me with new work at 1.30 am. He didn't seem to realise that I was only up because I was behind with the work. The last thing I needed was a new piece.

What is not recognised is that when you start, you have a limited customer base and work gets turned round fast, but having satisfied them early on, they demand the same quick service all the time. You just can't meet their demands.

I'd love the luxury of being ill.

☐ I've only had twelve days off sick in thirteen years. I can't afford to take time off. If you're not out there, you're not earning.

☐ When we'd been in business for about a year, one of my kids started to complain. "All you ever talk about is your business." We then made a conscious decision to talk about other things over the tea table. It's difficult though when you come home and all you can think about is what you have been doing all day. Me and my partner also noticed that at the end of the day we weren't asking each other "How are you?" but "How have you done?"

☐ What worries me most is the thought that I will lose my identity and become interested in the business and in little else.

☐ Before we opened our shop we went on the obligatory one day seminar about how to run a business. The man running the course said in a warning voice, "You have to put at least 35 hours a week into your business, you know."

The week we manage that I won't know what to do — 60 hours a week is the current average.

☐ My biggest outlay was the cost of the car and its maintenance. You go through a lot of clutches teaching people to drive. We did have a second car for a time, but we had a bump and it proved to be too expensive, so now I just run the one. Unless you're really big you're better off on your own. I work an average 30 - 35 hours a week, any more than that and I'm working for the tax man.

Pressing new buttons

☐ When government starts defining technology, separating new technology from technology, as it sometimes tries to, then it hits a can of worms. In engineering around here, there is little state of the art technology. What there is, is technical improvements to existing plant which amounts to major technical innovation. If an employer bolts a CNC to an existing drilling machine, one, say, which might be thirty years old, I would contend that the technology has advanced considerably and that the firm should be supported. To get into the big league and buy an up to date machine might cost a quarter of a million pounds. That would be new techology if you like. On the other hand, the innovation which is an adaptation of existing machinery is new technology to that business man and is achieving the same ends. Little buttons are getting pressed and the work place is becoming more efficient.

☐ There's a firm round here milling rods. There was probably a halfpenny profit on every one. You know, tuppence a bucket stuff. Each piece took about 1½ minutes to do. To improve productivity they took a machine from 1953, adapted it mechanically to produce a unit in 30 seconds — three times as fast as before. It's that type of incremental development which you are likely to see in this area, not something which is a major innovation.

☐ We have filled the work room with sayings which we hope the customers will notice. One reads "Bad planning on your part does not automatically constitute an automatic emergency on my part."

On from the penny mix

☐ A woman came into the shop and stood in front of me, slagging off shop keepers and their excessive profits. "Look," she said, "how much a lettuce costs and how much seeds cost."
"Madam," I said, "take this packet, try it, but for now, sod off."

☐ When you stock up you try to buy on the cheapest market and sell on the dearest, and that's why my husband used to come back from Scotland on a weekend with a suitcase filled with Lyon's pies.

So that we could keep our heads above the water when we were running the corner shop, Paul would go away to work very early on a Monday morning and come back on Friday evenings. It wasn't much of a life when you think of it. My hours were very long, his work meant that we didn't see each other and when we did, it was to push a trolley round a trade warehouse, stocking up. Profits such as they were, were marginal. You don't retire to the Costa Brava on the profits of a corner shop on the edge of a council estate.

There was one advantage though. The Scottish works canteen sold well packaged Lyon's pies at a highly subsidised price. I think they cost 5p when the recommended retail price was in the region of 20p. It was too much of an opportunity to miss. We bought him a long suitcase and made sure that he had plenty of change.

He reckons, though the story seems a little doubtful to me, that once, when he was negotiating the Scottish Customs at Berwick, a customs officer asked, "And what is in that suitcase, sir?"
"Pies," he replied.
They waved him through.

☐ It's reckoned that an inexperienced business man took a shop in a small local village. I was told it was Womersley but it might not have been. He did the shop up until it looked olde worlde and fitted the village to perfection.

The clientele, if anything, were a little refined, but all were anxious to support him. On the first morning the bell rang and in walked a tall, elegant lady.

"Good morning," she said, "I wonder if you have a packet of Lil-lets?"

"Well, I'll just have a look on here. No, I'm sorry, Rolos, Mintoes, Twirls and Wispas, but no Lil-lets."

☐ I never want to see a penny mix ever again. Jelly lips, mojos, milk teeth. I've seen the lot. Once I lost the cap off my tooth, I looked all over and then, when I got to the bottom of the milk teeth, there it was.

☐ Running a corner shop in Portobello, Wakefield, has to be one of the great unsung adventures of life. Customers are a case study in themselves. There was one woman who would come in, buy an onion, cut it and put a slice in her ear. She reckoned that it stopped wax. A lot would come and buy one onion, one egg and one oxo.

My fantasy was mounting a machine gun on the roof and mowing down all the people who wanted one egg, one slice of ham and those kids who couldn't quite make up their minds what to buy for the last penny and all the folk who waited till I locked the door of an evening, then nearly kicked the door in because they needed some cigs.

There was one who came in for an orange and as he was standing there, an enormous flea jumped off his head and landed on the counter. I was horrified, I didn't know what to do so I hit it with the nearest thing to hand which happened to be the orange, then handed it to him.

A profitable poet

☐ I must be the only poet who has made money out of his first published poem. My

Stephen McClarence

interest in local history prompted me to write a poem about the old shops in Station Lane as I remembered them from my childhood. After a time I had written some twenty stanzas and each one began with the same two words: "Who Remembers". Here's a verse to give you a flavour,

Who Remembers Gledhill's Top Shop
with three balls hung outside?
You could pawn your suit or wedding ring,
your mangle or your pride,
Your wore your suit at weekends,
then pawned it for a song,
Or enough to feed the family,
until pay day came along.

One day I went along to a meeting about old Featherstone and a chap I know, was reading from a book of tales from local folk. I thought that my poems might interest the meeting, but I couldn't pluck up the courage to read them. After the tea and biscuits however, I showed the poem to this bloke who, after a quick read, said he'd pass it on to a friend of his. His friend must have liked what he saw because a few days later he got in touch with me to ask if I'd like to see my poem in print. Well, at first, I wondered what it would entail; what would I have to do; how much would it cost me. After being assured that it would cost me nothing and after a soul searching two minutes, I agreed. The relatively small outlay for five hundred copies of a small booklet was to be borne by a couple of local people, one of them a local M.P. who would obviously expect to be reimbursed if and when the books were sold. Were they backing the favourite or a rank outsider? I very much hoped I could prove the former.

Here I was in the publishing game but it was not as easy as it looked. First I had to brush up the verses and decide what line spacing I wanted. There were only eight pages and the title, Who Remembers Featherstone, was at the top of the first page, along with two stanzas. It couldn't have been more basic.

A local printer agreed to do all the stages, setting out, printing and stapling, for the princely sum of £62. Five hundred copies cost twelve and a half pence each. That in technical jargon is called the unit cost. Now we had to decide how much to charge for the booklet and how and where we would sell it. We decided on a price of twenty pence, which in hindsight was underpriced. I was fortunate in having a friend with a busy shop who agreed to sell them for me. Equally fortunately, there was a play about old Featherstone running in the local community centre and I was able to sell my poems at the show.

I have to admit that the pile of five hundred copies in my front room caused me to start having second thoughts, but it was too late. I forced the first few copies onto my friends and much to my surprise and pleasure, they suddenly took off. My shop-keeper friend couldn't get enough of them and the week of the play, I must have sold over half.

I jokingly asked my friends if they wanted signed copies and before I knew it, everyone wanted them. Fame at last. Most people have to wait until they are dead. I had five hundred copies on Monday morning and by Friday, I had paid off my friends and was into profit. This was clear profit of course as I had no labour costs. In a very few weeks, I had sold out. My local Historical Society kindly decided to sponsor a reprint which sold very well. In fact, copies are now hard to come by and I am a profitable poet.

Many people asked me if I had any plans to do another improved edition, so I thought, why not. This time, along with another sponsor, we decided to do this better book. Using the skills I had learned and with some new verses, I set about the task. We decided this time on better paper, some old photographs, a bit of colour, a title page and introduction. I learned how to cut and paste, that is to paste the verses into a mock-up of the book and then to design the front cover. With a photo of me on the back cover and a little bit about me, we had a good, presentable book. I took the mock-up

Stephen McClarence

along to the typesetter myself and after some difficult proof reading and photo cutting, I had something reasonable for the printer.

Now came the expected crunch. The cost for five hundred copies was about £450 instead of £62. After much discussion, we decided on a price of £1 per copy. This was a much smaller profit margin and we would have to sell a lot more before the investor got his money back. The book has sold very well but over a longer period of time. My sponsor has been repaid but as sales slow down, the profit to me comes in dribs and drabs. I expect to sell them all eventually, but I often wonder if another small booklet would have been more profitable in the long run. I suppose I'll never know.

On a marketing training course, recently, I asked people what they would pay for each of my books. Surprisingly, all of them would have paid fifty pence or a pound for the small book, but only a little more than a pound for the big one. There must be a lesson there somewhere.

Perhaps if I had done more market research before I began, things may have been different. But then, I was only a beginner.

Stephen McClarence

Stephen McClarence

☐ If you had a new idea, a boat taking passengers down an industrial stretch of a river, then Coal Board Enterprises could not see its potential for jobs. There were no precedents. There was nothing to base judgement on. York had trip boats but that wasn't totally applicable, that was an established tourist spot.

If you were doing a bit of coal leading, buying a milk round and going into window cleaning, they would find money for that. Yet when you said that you were situated yards from, and in easy view of, one of Britain's principal motorways, it seemed to be irrelevant to them. They wouldn't recognise that jobs would be created in catering on the boat and at the Golden Lion, and that we will be employing someone to do the administration and run the booking office. They had no barometer and they lacked vision. The regulations were too narrow gutted. The British Coal Enterprise Scheme would only look at schemes which would "create full time employment for people" and although Mr Thacker at the Five Towns Enterprise Centre was helpful and taught us a lot about the accounting side, they didn't give any support even though I was a redundant miner who was creating work in the coalfield. That was because they lacked vision.

☐ After the pit closed, we were both told that the area would be used by the Coal Board as one of its so called Enterprise Parks. At the time it seemed a right good thing, the pit had gone and here was something that would bring some hope back into the community. It was the *Caring* Coal Board this time.

People risked their savings and put their homes on the line to set up small businesses at the end of Station Lane. Then British Coal sold it without consultation. They pulled the rug from under people's feet.

☐ We decided we would like to start our own business when we heard about the

British Coal Enterprise Scheme, which was to be set up on the site of the old colliery. I had spent my working life as a steel erector but I always took local jobs. I couldn't see any point in having a family and hardly ever seeing them. My wife worked in the clothing industry and had a lot of experience so we decided to run the business together.

We chose this unit because it was light and airy and because it was a lot tidier than the other units. The rest of the site was a mess which meant that a lot of preparatory work needed doing before we could get started. We financed the business ourselves from our savings. The bank was no help to start with. The Wakefield Council gave us a grant of £1,000 and granted us a loan of £1,000 after one year of trading. I also got £40 pounds a week from the Enterprise Board.

The break came when I saw there was an opening on the market for riding breeches, with people having more leisure time and horse riding being available to all classes. Times had changed since we were young when riding was only for the well-off and farmers' children. To make sure I was right I researched the market by writing to sports shops and riding schools. The response was fair but there were no direct answers until people had seen the product. We made samples and posted them to prospective customers who seemed satisfied with the quality of our work.

Now we have a nice steady business going, with no cash flow problems. I get cash on delivery apart from a few customers who are too far away to deliver personally. The bank now lets us have overdraft facilities. We have proved that we can make a go of it.

British Coal were no help at all, there was too much red tape. If we had relied on them, I doubt if we now would have four full-time and three part-time workers. We get a council grant for two girls, but we don't bother with Y.T.S. students. Originally we had some but it didn't work out because the disparity in pay affects their attitude to the job. When they are expected to do the same work for their grant as the other workers who are earning a lot more, they get resentful. Then there's the problem of them becoming an extra pair of hands because when the scheme ends, they have to be replaced by a well-paid worker.

When this site was up for sale, all the tenants wanted to get together and buy it in a partnership with the council, but British Coal sold it from under our feet. We don't know who our new landlords are, but we do know they are a London insurance company. It was sold for £470,000.

We have adapted to a completely new way of life, a new environment and new type of work and we enjoy it, but now we are being faced with big electricity bills, so we want to leave. The British Coal agreement was that the cost of the electricity was included in the rent, now we are faced with a bill for £1,200 for the whole of the block. Quite a few people have moved out either to other premises or they have packed in altogether.

We have expanded our range and now make rugby jerseys. I would like to open a shop and sell a wider choice of sportswear and have the factory above the shop.

We will be happy to get our own place. Rent is just dead money.

Regulations rule O.K.

☐ The council is far from clear about the way council houses can be used as business premises. In Sheffield, as I understand it, there is a much more thought through policy. I'm not sure if this is a virtue or not. They must know that kitchen trading goes on. Women for generations have sold wedding cakes from the home.

In any case, the bottom end of the market is difficult to define. Is a woman who sells through a Littlewood's catalogue trading; is a collector of football pools in business? I suspect that the whole area is such a minefield that they turn a blind eye. Mind, if you became a subsidiary of British Nuclear Fuels something might be said. On the other hand, they might not even notice.

☐ The problem with a lot of small family

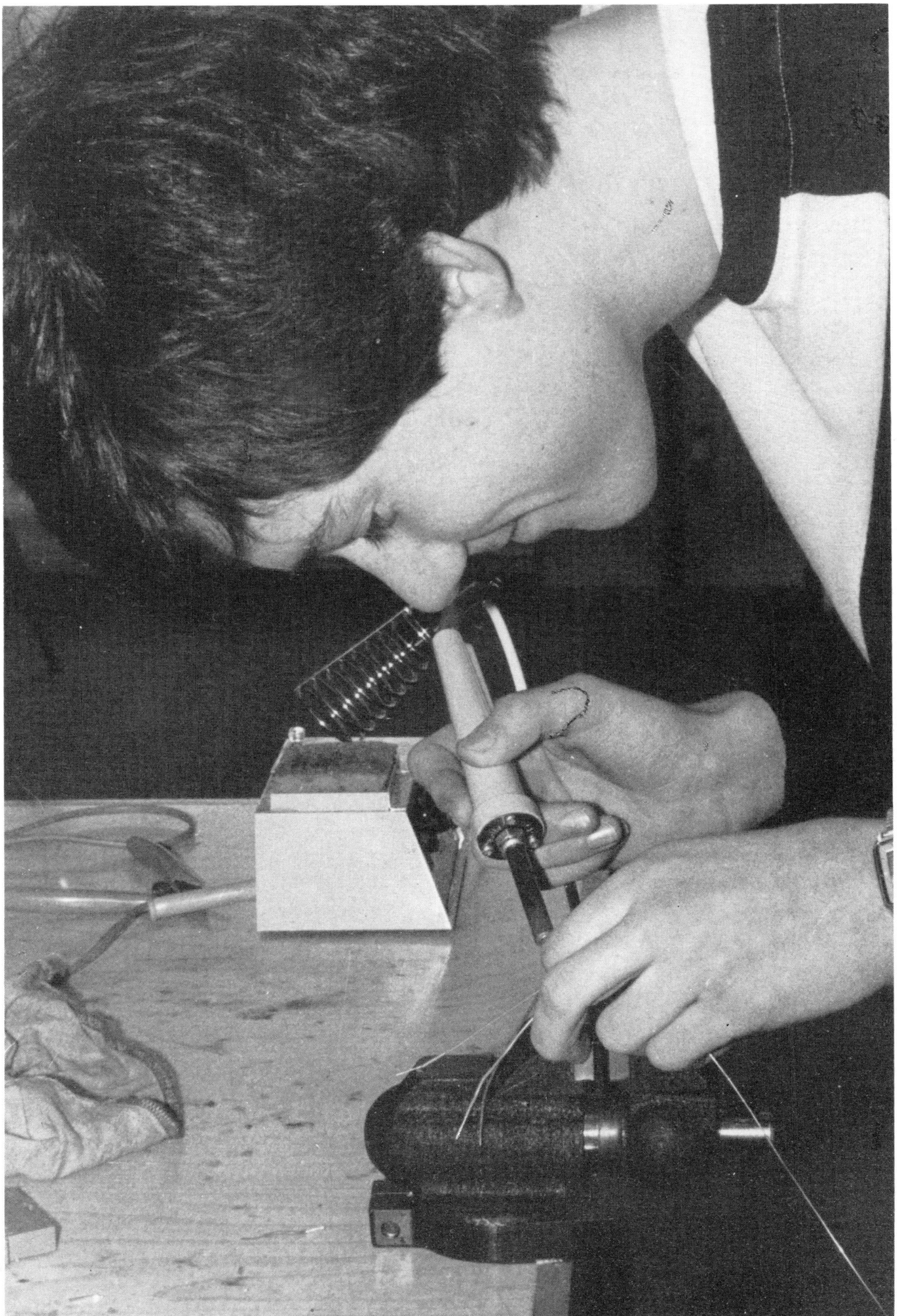

Mike Petty

businesses is that they can't or won't keep up with the times. Rules and regulations change, particularly in the chemical industry, and businesses have to adapt. One man I went to advise told me that if he accepted my recommendations, he would end up closing down the factory. "All I need now," he said, "is a visit from the Water Authority telling me I'm polluting the river." Half an hour later, while I was still sitting there, that is exactly what happened.

☐ When you set up a business, it is essential that you take into account the money that complying with government regulations will cost you.

Involvement with the Department of Trade and Industry can knock a real hole in your pocket; they are very expensive to talk to. For instance, if they have to come to Ferrybridge from Hull it is £42 an hour.

Government agencies know how to charge for labour costs. Of course if we worked out of Leeds Canal Basin it would cost even more because that's sixteen miles further on.

Then you have to make decisions about the inspection itself. I knew enough about this boat and its engine to strip it down myself. I have always messed about in boats and am a qualified fitter from my coal mining days, but I knew that on balance they would prefer to deal with an established yard and so I took it into a dry dock in Goole and had an established marine engineering firm look at it. That set us back, if you take into consideration their £1,500 dry dock and licensing costs over £2,000. We are hardly the big time. That is a lot of money.

☐ Given a year or two and even middle sized companies won't subcontract to small companies without knowing that they have got British Standard 5750. Consequently companies who do not have the British Standard for Quality assurance will lose work. Now British Coal, British Rail and YEB are insisting that you have 5750 clearance before you get a contract. All things being equal, any serious company will work with the ones who have got 5750.

It's a vital qualification in any negotiation. Companies having got computerised now want everything documented in a manual. Before you know it, there's a whole world of small businesses creating quality control manuals. It's generally recognised that you need systems which can tell you at any one moment when a part came in, how it was used on such-and-such a day and which piece of equipment accepted it. In the end they come to identify whole interchangeable systems. That's British Standards for you. Every aspect of a job is going to be more sophisticated from now on.

Firms without 5750 will get nowhere, for they will be forced to stay at the bottom of the market. They won't get into Europe and as more companies acquire 5750 status, they will be left behind. You see 5750 is an attitude of mind which eventually will affect even the really small businesses.

☐ The sinking of that pleasure boat in the Thames brought in a whole range of regulations. They have cost us a little money but it has been worth it. Now we don't start a voyage without recording the number of people on board and making sure that the record is left ashore. We have also improved the internal communication system.

I'm not complaining. All that is to the good. It's also had positive advantages because it's made us see that we need an on-shore office both for bookings and to help out the new system. If anything, it has accelerated a policy which was developing slowly.

☐ By-laws pertaining to hygiene have not been too difficult because at my shop we only decorate the cakes, so all we need is a sink to ensure washing facilities for our basic tools. Health Inspectors do pop up to the bungalow because I do all the cooking there and the hygiene laws are more stringent there, but so far I have passed all the requirements. I learned all about hygiene in the course at college and I have considerable knowledge on bacteria and poisons.

☐ To begin a venture it is easier to have

a partner, so when Gill and I met at the ante-natal and our friendship grew we both realised that we should get together our talents as teacher and promotions manager and set ourselves up in the catering business. After much research around 'Fat Freds' and 'MacDonalds' in Leeds we took the plunge and here we are at the 'Granary Cafe' under the Dark Arches in Leeds. When we moved on 1st May 1990, it had been an existing cafe and we had to redesign and put our own stamp on the place and so far it has been very successful. We home bake on the premises because hygiene laws forbid us to do so at home. From now on new legislation will mean that many foods will have to be chilled.

☐ This is reckoned to be the largest Wool Stapler's Warehouse in Europe, but since it has been a listed building, the insurance has gone up 650%. That's a big increase in two years and a lot of money to find. We're competing with the big stores down on Dewsbury Road and although their furniture prices are 12½% over and above ours, they are more accessible.

☐ Planning is killing this town, planning and planners. They reckon that this area is to become all little craft shops. You know the sort of thing, old women tatting, and a man shoeing a horse. All they've managed to do so far is take over more and more land to park their cars.

☐ The big boys on the outskirts have to turn over £30,000 a week to break even. Now I believe you cannot do that for long. So what's the future? A town with a street of banks and building societies, a tourist quarter and the lot surrounded by big empty warehouses.

☐ In the east end of Sheffield they are building Europe's biggest shopping complex. That's alright I suppose, but it's not much good to an old lady who wants two ounce of potted meat for her tea.

People used to earn wages on the site of that shopping Mall — steelworkers. Now they'll go in there and come out skint. You can't run an economy on shopping centres and Leisure Domes. You need proper jobs; making things — that's real wealth creation.

Not allowing for enterprise

☐ I'm a self taught artist and for years I'd been doing portraits for friends. Eighteen months ago I decided to try and make a living from my paintings. My husband wanted to get out of the rat race he was in with his job, so we decided to set up together. To go on the Enterprise Allowance we had to raise £2,000 and this was very frustrating. It took us over a year because no one was prepared to lend us money as we didn't have a house to put up as security.

I spend the time going round play schools and craft fairs persuading people to buy my portraits. This was useful because it meant that when we finally opened a shop, I was known and people felt they could drop in for a chat.

☐ The problem with a lot of people involved in the Enterprise Allowance Scheme (EAS) is that many of the applicants gear themselves to getting £40 a week and really have no passionate interest in getting into business. The people who they first meet also set a tone which is wholly wrong. Their interest is meeting a target, and consequently the wish to set up a business is enough. In this area there was not even an elementary form to fill in. Wishing is not enough. You need training and a business plan. There are no tried systems, no support and no serious vetting. Money goes down a hole and no one seriously monitors the size of the hole. The only thing that can be said is that only one in five recipients of EAS is in business three years after starting up.

☐ A lot of people try it on because there are so many grants available for small businesses. One guy applied for a grant from the Isle of Man Government to develop a fuel saving device; he also applied for a grant from the D.T.I. for marketing it. It was supposed to link into a boiler and save fuel by generating negative ions. He claimed to have 'scientific proof', none of which could be corroborated, but he'd persuaded at least two large companies to attach his device to their boilers to save energy. I spent six hours listening to him while he chain-smoked. I still don't know to this day if the Isle of Man knew what they were funding.

☐ They didn't teach us much about business skills at our college, although the course was supposed to be vocation orientated. We had about 1½ hours a week for two years but the bits they did were about mortgages and things like that. It was not practical at all and taught us nothing we need to know now we are out here working.

They were training designers for the High Street shops and not giving us an opportunity to go into business on our own account. Of course the trainers know nothing about small businesses themselves. You have to have run a small business to understand it.

☐ This area has a long tradition of early school leaving and minimal training, which they have to overcome now that low-skill jobs are disappearing. There is also a lack of entrepreneurial tradition which discourages the growth of new industries.

There is a need to improve training to make the workforce more adaptable. Manufacturers themselves will have to become more adaptable and responsive to changing technology and market conditions.

Training has been improving steadily, but whether it has done more than prevent the gap with our competitors from widening still further is open to doubt. There are also some major gaps. Most provision is concentrated on young people and those with higher skills. There is little long-term planning to meet business needs. Only 19% of training establishments tried to assess the benefits of the training they had undertaken

Stephen McClarence

and only 3% tried to measure benefits against costs.

☐ I went on an MSC course in 1973 called "Your Redundancy Problem". The lectures were given by a young man, well intentioned but wet behind the ears. One of the subjects covered was preparing for interview. "Take the opportunity to be personally comfortable," he said "Visit the toilet and wash your hands." I saw red. At 42 with two full business careers behind me, to be told to wash your hands by a 23 year old. I walked out.

I went straight to the course director's office and demanded to know who vetted the course content and who vetted the poor 23 year old. "Your next course on redundancy," I said, "I will run it for free. And the one after that you will pay me for." That's how I started in business as a tutor consultant; anger was the trigger.

☐ At a high class seminar run by Leeds Polytechnic, an eminent scholar, a specialist on economic theory, was trying to persuade his audience to purchase an academic journal about the theory of business. He went on for some time until I could stand it no longer. Although the bulk of the questions were about infra-structure and macro-economics — high tone subjects, I asked straight out, "Where are the earlier numbers of this book you are wanting us to invest in?"

"I sorry," he said, "I forgot to bring them."

There he was lecturing us on the theory of economics and marketing and he hadn't got the nouse to have his wares set out.

I wouldn't buy anything from him if I saw him selling down on Leeds Market.

Pin money and proper jobs

☐ I once heard a council officer tear into a woman from an unemployment centre, telling her that the jobs which she was creating were not jobs at all; that they were little better than pin-money hobbies. That attitude annoyed me. There she was in a safe pensionable employment with views on strategy which suggested that the only jobs worth considering were full-time ones.

Had she never heard of dual economies? There would have been no first industrial revolution if Calderdale farmers, who couldn't support themselves as farmers, hadn't seen the benefit of supplementing their incomes by doing a bit of spinning and weaving on the side. Enterprise comes from jobs which have sound footings. It's better to have two part time jobs than no job at all.

When I started in 1980 I had six different sources of income. Not one of them amounted to a full time job, but put together they added up to something.

☐ A study of West Yorkshire by the University of Louvain concludes that too high a proportion of European Regional Development Fund grants to the county goes to infrastructure projects (86%) and not enough to initiatives to develop productive industries more directly (14%). So far as the European Social Fund is concerned many of us believe that too high a proportion continues to go to UK government schemes and too little to local initiatives.

☐ The council does not see the whole answer to unemployment being the encouragement of small firms or the enterprise culture, like the Government does. The Government has stolen the words "enterprise" and "choice" but we believe that by offering a range of policies and hopefully a range of solutions, people will have more choice. That includes the choice to be an entrepreneur or to work for someone else. We aim for long-term, sustainable, good quality jobs with transferable skills.

☐ What with the Enterprise Allowance, Enterprise Initiative and Enterprise Parks springing up all over the place, people now have a very narrow view of what 'enterprise' means. They only see it as 'business' — start a business, make something, sell it, make

Stephen McClarence

a profit and bugger everything/anybody else. Anything that doesn't conform to this isn't seen as a real job or real work.

This is one view; it obviously works, look round Castleford. There are people who have made it work. But what about all the other ways you can be enterprising? Anybody on a low income has to be enterprising just to make ends meet.

Having enterprise to me means having ideas, imagination, the ability to make those ideas work, solving problems and learning from what you do. Learning something for the sake of it or because you think it might be useful sometime. I think it is sad if you feel that to be enterprising you have to see immediate results every time, or turn in a quick profit. I know we all have to earn a living, but there are a lot of ways of combining being enterprising with earning a living.

I remember when I was about sixteen, I decided I wanted to be either a sculptor, a photographer or write comedy for the BBC. The careers' teacher said "And what will you do for a proper job?" I haven't yet had the courage to follow my ideas, so seventeen years on here I am, working for the council, trying to put something back into the community I was born into. I have to be very enterprising in my work; some people might think that's very odd for a council officer.

Head down, arse up and you can't see the world around you

HEAD DOWN, ARSE UP AND DON'T LOOK ROUND

Styles of Management

Pitching it right

☐ Selling can be quite frightening at first. Lots of people make the assumption that if you can make something, you can sell it. I really felt as though I was putting myself on the line when I first set up our stall at fairs and fetes. I'd be on one side and on the other would be a huge general public. They were looking at something I'd made, but 99 times out of 100 they would reject it.

All four of us found this quite soul destroying until we discovered that the best way to sell is to make it entertaining. If you turn selling into theatre and start telling people stories, you can soon draw a crowd and get them buying. You have to give people an excuse for why they need your product. When I'm selling our jewellery, I'm not just selling an object, I'm selling the intangible, the story behind it.

☐ When two of us had enough money, we employed a friend who knew little about the trade, to market our books in the local area and eventually in Yorkshire as a whole. It was a gamble, but it paid off. She had recently separated from her husband who had said as he departed "You! You couldn't earn a thing. In fact for every pound you make I'll put a fiver on top of it." His contempt linked with her need to make a bit extra cash made her fearless. From being an underrated housewife she became our book representative. She loved it, she had a natural way with people and quickly built up a good network. We had had a bad experience two years previously when we had sent out books to a professional repping service. They took 55% of the cover price, demanded that they had sole selling rights in the bookshops of the area and then only managed to sell 17 copies of one title.

Our new rep reversed the trend, our books began to sell all over. We couldn't afford much promotional material but what bits we had, she made use of. I began to see our name all over the place. I once went into a local pub and behind the bar, close to the Bells' Whisky and the Hamlet Cigars, there were our books.

☐ Every piece of jewellery I design has to have a hook — it needs to make someone feel they are a viking, in the civil war or whatever; we are appealing to the romance in people. In all the history books, I've noticed that in the last decade of every century, people go backward and start getting interested in old costumes and jewellery. At the end of each millenium, people go even more beserk, so for us 1990 is really good news. Of course in ten years time we will have to radically alter our product because everyone will start to go futuristic.

☐ These are the best markets you'll find anywhere in the country. The Barnsley one, they reckon, used to be better. That was until the council got its hands on it and put it indoors.

Markets advertise themselves but good traders have to work at it. There's a number of stages you go through. Unless you've been born into market work, and I wasn't, then you stand behind a stall and wait for people to speak to you. The next stage you speak to them and finally if you are good at selling the right thing you "pitch."

Pitchers can make real money. The good ones don't live in houses, they live in mansions. I suppose that Joe Edwards was the best known Yorkshire one. He made a fortune juggling plates in Barnsley Market and ended up as Master of Hounds. It's often in crockery — pots, plates — that you get the best pitchers. That's because there are always a lot of things that you can give away, like cruets which cost you pence. A crowd will always gather if something is being given away free.

☐ In the market I choose what to play so that it will attract people. The repertoire, if you want to call it that, is popular. *Knees Up Mother Brown* to *The Merry Widow* via *Show Me The Way To Go Home.* Mind, you cannot get much out of this type of keyboard and this power system. I go all over the country playing. The overheads are low, transport really.

Any day I'll make £40 minimum, but if I sell a couple of tapes at £4.50 each, that's where the profit comes from. Blank tapes in boxes cost 70p a time and you need to buy in studio recording time. For me that's in Chesterfield, but my home base isn't here in Pontefract but in Sheffield. The colour printing for 500 covers is about £100, so as you can see, the complete package has been put together for about £500. That's a unit total of approximately £1 per tape. The mark up isn't bad in those terms because for the last few weeks I have run out of colour labels and am having to make do with photocopies.

☐ I have taken to setting up a table outside the shop with a photographic album carrying pictures of all of my cakes. On the cover I have printed "Please take a look inside." Sometimes it backfires because people come in and having seen something I made in the past and insist on wholly unrealistic additions. On the other hand they do stop and look. I think that is a much more cost effective way of selling yourself than an advertisement in the newspaper.

☐ When I don't have too much work coming in to be done, I advertise in our local paper for typing to be done at home. It costs in the region of £3.05 each time and the first time I advertised, I got work that brought in about £32. The time after, I didn't get any jobs at all. I have had some cards printed and they have brought in a fair amount of typing, but word of mouth has brought in the most work.

One day I dropped off some complete typing and was given another letter to type and a book to be enclosed with the letter. I hadn't taken a bag with me, so I had to keep the book and handwritten draft in my hand. I called in a nearby shop for a sandwich on my way back home and the shopkeeper said, "Somebody looks as if they are going to be busy." I explained that I took in typing to be done at home and she asked me how much I would charge to do her some typing. That day I went home with three lots of typing and the promise of more as she required it.

☐ Do you realise that there are only three big concerns in the funeral business; the Co-op, Hodgson Holdings, and the Southern Group; and that they have bought up the rest but have kept the little firms' names? They have to, you see, you don't get far in this business until your name means something. What the big companies buy up are respect and reputation. Who has ever heard of a new funeral director? People say "They've buried me mum so they'll bury me." Twenty years can pass between funerals. Reputations are made by word of mouth, not elaborate advertising.

Today a hearse with one car costs at basic around £600. In 1957 you could get six cars for £43. Inflation has been bad but not like that. If you could get in the business there is a fortune to be made, but it is difficult to break through, even if you have the necessary skills to do the job.

☐ A leaflet came through the door this morning. TEA UP WITH THE COWBOYS it said. I read on further and discovered it was actually a painter and decorator looking for business. The gothic lettering they had

Stephen McClarence

gone in for was so bad that FED UP looked like TEA UP. When people discover there is more than one way to lay out a leaflet they go mad. Word processor packages with a lot of complicated type faces have a lot to answer for.

☐ I've not done much local advertising, relying on word of mouth recommendations, but that is because I always felt that I wouldn't find many customers in Featherstone itself. The bulk of people I had contacted up to the time I took the small ad in the Featherstone Advertiser, were the type of people who wanted last year's garment altered to fit this year's figure and were prepared to pay next to nothing to have it done. They were the customers I could do without. However at £16 with a small picture in the front page, bottom corner, I couldn't afford to miss. It attracted quite a lot of attention and as a result, my local custom has developed.

I travel all over — Shipley, Bradford, Leeds — doing garment parties and I will tell you this, I've met few nicer people than I have met in Featherstone. Two local women phoned up and because I liked the sound of them; happy, down to earth, I decided to give it a go. Most of my customers are middle class, but they are no better spenders than those women and their friends.

Some *designers* wouldn't have risked a night there. They want to sell to the "£150-a-blouse" market. Not me. But then, although I am well qualified, I prefer to call myself a dress maker rather than a designer.

Selling yourself

☐ It is difficult to know where to look when you want a partner. Some will tell you that quiet people and noisy ones don't mix. In our experience we get on very well. I am always going off with a new idea and Graham is more steady. If he sees something won't work he says so and he's often right, but usually he will see the potential if the idea is good.

He's the practical one. He can strip the engine down if he needs to, skipper the boat and see to routine things. Two years ago he was a successful fitter at Allerton Bywater. I am more mouthy and come from a different background. I've been twenty years self-employed in building and groups so I see the importance of advertising and projection. This allows us to get publicity free by giving the newspapers and television a story to bite on. For instance, Viv Nicholson, who is my sister, will be doing a programme from the boat in July and I expect the Yorkshire Art Circus to come onto the boat to do one of their book collecting days after that.

☐ I lost my first partner because she got fed up with what she saw as the deadening lack of enterprise which she found in the north and went off to London. I had lived there so I didn't have illusions about the wonderful London scene. She was looking for something different from me, both psychologically and socially. I think that you can say that she couldn't take the pressure. Put simply I think that she was looking for an arts experience whereas I wanted to build a business.

My new partner, we've been together for a year, is different. He loves the north and we complement each other.

☐ I run my own record company and therefore make a living from an artform, but if I had to put my hand up, I'd have to say that business and art just do not mix. For one thing you can't make any money out of it and for another these musicians are so bloody temperamental. Don't get me wrong, when there is business to make out of art, I've absolutely no qualms about making some. I'll consider the art once I've made my profit. But then again I might hear something one day that I think other people ought to hear and I'll release it for artistic reasons, that's my business.

☐ She's a Taurus and I'm a Virgo. I take on the technical side and she does what she's good at, communicates well with people and is our mouthpiece. I'm systematic and therefore suited to video recording.

Our break came when Economic Development showed some faith in us. I think that the future of the arts is working through that type of department as long as it's far sighted. To succeed you need notions about business practice and to have thought through some of the basic problems. The best thing we ever did was to go on a four week intensive training course for graduates at Huddersfield Polytechnic. It didn't teach us how to get out of any one bad situation but it taught us to know when we had a problem.

☐ If I tried to sell the business I don't suppose I'd get much for it, just the price of the car. What I'd be trying to sell is myself, I am the business, people come here because they like me, not my car. Having said that, you do need a car, people like to drive. We once tried a diesel engine, but it was very easy to stall on a hill start and that puts people off. They say, "I'm not going to him, his car is horrible."

☐ When we first opened the shop, I thought that people would buy my pictures because they liked them. What I found out was that people want to know who you are before they'll buy. I also learned about how to attract people into my shop. I assumed that my customers would want to see my pictures through the window so I kept the window display space clear. Then I realised everyone was looking through the window but no one was actually coming in. I filled the windows with cards and posters and within minutes, people were coming in and browsing around. My sales then doubled.

☐ When we first opened the shop, my daughter Josephine hadn't started school. She used to come with me every day and sit in the corner, drawing and painting. One day a customer was browsing through my

Kevin Reynolds

Kevin Reynolds

pictures when she stopped and came up to my desk. "What's this?" she asked with a smile. She was holding one of Josephine's pictures — a painting of a horse with the sign £21 scrawled in the corner.

Another time Josephine left my shop and went next door to where they make wedding dresses. She presented them with a drawing and said in a loud voice, "It's alright, I won't charge you for it."
I hadn't realised until then how much of the sales language she was picking up.

☐ No customers seem dissatisfied and at the moment we are doing typesetting and layout for some really big companies. Of course they are not fully sure of the quality of the work so I say, "Look here, If you really want something different I am prepared to slick down my hair, put a gold ring through my ear; Julie will put on a mini skirt and we will buy a couple of tubs full of potted plants and set up in the centre of Leeds. Of course the work won't be different, its just that we will charge you three times this much for coming through the door and then we will start looking at the cost of the job."

I'll do a job for £50. If they went to Leeds they would start talking at £200, yet I am not sure if some of them wouldn't prefer to pay that. Image means a lot to some companies.

A champion

☐ You get two sorts of entrepreneur. The first type is usually a man in his early thirties with management experience. He's either been made redundant or else he finds himself in a rut and knows he won't get further as he is. He's possibly hit the thirtieth birthday crisis. One day he decides to go for gold. He uses his house as equity and sets up by himself. His approach is thought through and systematic. If he has become redundant he usually has the confidence to believe that he could find another job and uses the redundancy money as a

Stephen McClarence

windfall which supplies him with capital he would not have had before. He has probably come from a smallish firm.

Then there's the other type. He's born to be an entrepreneur. He probably started off by selling sweets in the playground and building up his capital in a post office savings book. It would probably be the post office because at ten he'd be aware of the income tax implications if it goes into a building society. By the time he's twenty he knows exactly where he's going.

☐ It's a word you hear sometimes in business — entrepreneur. I looked it up in the dictionary the other day. It gave two rather flat meanings and another which was a bit special. It said Entrepreneur (Fr): "an agent, an undertaker." Then it said "a champion."

☐ We ran a competition in 1988 for new businesses as part of Wakefield's centenary celebrations. It was called *Success 88.* Well I asked this young business man to enter. He wouldn't. He said that although it was true that he would almost certainly win, and he was right there, it was not the image he wanted to create. He wanted people to think his was a long established business and not one which had been going for just two years. He was thinking long term.

☐ There's a local firm which imports condoms from the Far East and packages them for sale in this country. Now you might argue that a condom is a condom. He'd say that you were wrong. It could be coloured, it could be flavoured. He has seen the gap in the market. He's only in his thirties now, yet he drives a Porsche. He started with two people doing packaging from his flat.

☐ There's a little tea shop in Hemsworth opposite the church that is doing really well. This school teacher reckoned that you could run a tea shop there so he cleared out downstairs and moved upstairs. It's really small, I doubt if there are more than six tables but everything is spotless. They sell vegetarian food as well as normal food.

☐ I can tell you two stories from our pit. Two brothers worked on pumps and took to studying them. In the end they reckoned that they could make one better so they did and took out a patent. Now they are in the position that they could sell the rights to an American Company.

Another fella and his wife set up a tea-cum-tuck shop. She was called Maureen and he was Alan. They called it *The Alamo.*

☐ The belief that money can be made out of writing and publishing is widespread. It would amaze you how many people come forward with ideas about books. I always tell them the same thing, "Any fool can print and publish a book, the difficult thing is selling one."

There's a cut-off point, you see, somewhere around two hundred, after which, having sold the book to relatives and friends, you are on your own. That's when the enterprise starts. Unfortunately this is well below the 500 print run which is the minimum edition you should think about when you go to a printer. I have to admit though that I have seen people make money on books in situations where I wouldn't have rated their chances at all.

One winter's night the Yorkshire Art Circus launched a book in Calderdale about a Russian woman's travels through Europe in the 1930s and 1940s. It was called *From Vladivostok To Halifax.* It sold well I understand in both towns but didn't do much in between. Most of Nina Holland's English friends were Salvationists — not a group I associate with book buying — but at the launch they dutifully purchased a copy, lined up for Nina to sign it and then stood around eating and drinking the refreshments we had provided.

As I drifted from one group to another, as you do at such gatherings, I noticed a woman in her sixties moving about in an altogether more purposeful way. She would go to a group, press a small book on them, take money and move on. It didn't take much to get in her line of flight. In a minute or two she was talking to me.

"Would you like to buy my poetry book. It's in dialect and is called *Med I' Halifax* and costs £1.50."

It was a well rehearsed patter, but I was intrigued and parted with the money. The book itself was staple sewn, not particularly well printed. Anyone with a bit of experience could see that it had been put together by a jobbing printer with little knowledge of book production. It probably cost no more than 40p to produce, so if you avoid reckoning in her labour costs, she was making £1.10 per copy. Not bad.

"Do you sell many?" I asked. For years I had preached that there was only a poor market for poetry and virtually no market for dialect poetry, therefore her answer surprised me.

"Well, I printed 2000 for this second edition after I had sold the first edition of 1000 books. I printed less of the first book, I think I did 1500."

The sums are relatively easy. Put the two books together and assume a common selling price. Her turnover when all books were sold was in the region of £6,700. Her outlay must have been something less than £1,200. Not a bad profit and all she needed, apart from the initial poetic inspiration, was a dry space to store her books and a large carrier bag.

Mind I am still unrepentant and continue to preach that dialect poetry won't make the bestseller lists. In my book she is the exception that proves the rule.

Think what she did. She invaded someone else's book launch, eyeballed people and got not wholly sympathetic strangers to part with cash. She succeeded because she had an inordinate amount of cheek. That's some achievement. Good luck to her I say.

☐ When this particular operator heard that the firm he had bought the Rusk Dyeing Machine from was heading for the rocks he acted quickly. The £14,000 machine was not paid for, so he immediately slapped in a demand for repair and sent invoices for broken parts worth upwards of £10,000. When the receiver came in he saw the bill and the repairs charges. He argued that it was not worth trying collecting the difference and wrote off the debt. That's one way to get a new machine for nothing.

☐ This man bought an old-fashioned foundry and saw there was a niche in the market for specialised steels, so he put in money. He's now taking more people on in a non-ferrous foundry making things for minesweepers. That's not in Portsmouth, that's in Wakefield.

☐ My first business was at the age of 7 years. My father chopped a wheelbarrow full of firewood and told me to sell it. Well, off I went, barely strong enough to push the barrow, but sold the wood for twopence a bucketful along the first row of houses. At that I dashed back home jangling nine old pennies in my pocket. I was thrilled to bits. I sold lots of wood after that but gave it up when Dad made me chop the wood myself. I found this too difficult.

My second business venture was when I was 28. I had just started my teaching career and I was desperately hard up. I took a market stall on Normanton market and sold ribbon, cotton and needles. It was not very successful because these goods were slow sellers. I found the job very cold and it was also boring when business was slack. I gave the stall up when I got a teaching post at Normanton Grammar School.

After three years at Bradford University on a Maths Degree course I got a post at Scarborough Technical College and bought a house. This meant I was heavily in debt and could not obtain any extra work. My luck seemed to change when I got the chance to take over a second hand shop for a year. It was a tight thing. I paid the last £100 in the bank for all the stock and the first month's £2-10 shillings a week rent.

My first purchase was an old sofa and a very ancient wind-up gramophone in a beautiful inlaid cabinet. I didn't have any transport so I fetched the goods on an old

Stephen McClarence

pram. I took the old gramophone straight round to the Lindy Lou Antique Shop. I got £7 for it, a lot of money in those days. The old sofa I sold one week later for £3. Gradually I began to discriminate between junk and genuine antiques. I became really interested in old coins. Once I remember I bought The King's Shilling. That cost £6.

☐ During the pit dispute this guy had lots of time on his hands. Remember at this time the area was filled with professionals making television programmes about the strike. At the end of the dispute he took redundancy. Although a colliery fitter, he had fiddled about with videos and saw a gap in the market. When new machinery is put into place, manuals usually accompany delivery, but he recognised that training videos were a better proposition. He started out as a colliery fitter. Today he has got into the big time. Now he's doing work for Channel Four. You don't have to remain where you start from.

Nineteen with no mortgage

☐ Although I am only nineteen and had anticipated being made redundant, when the news finally came I had extremely mixed feelings. I was desperate for a career change. I wanted something exciting to happen to my life but it never seemed the opportune moment to do anything about it. On the other hand, I had never been made redundant before and did not want to become another government statistic. I was going to grab this opportunity and at least attempt to make a go of something constructive. I had been working for an Employment Agency for two and a half years, my first job since leaving school. I had really enjoyed working closely with the public and feeling I was doing my bit for society. There are approximately thirty other staff agencies in the city. My company was long established and was still run on very traditional lines. I was ready to change my old fashioned ink quill for a streamline pen yet no matter how much enthusiasm I mustered, or how many bright suggestions I put to the board, I felt as though I was hitting my head against a brick wall. My company's get up and go had gone a long time ago.

A decision had to be made. I never intended to spend the rest of my life in the same job. I wasn't going to turn round at 45 and say "If only I had done something different with my life!" The idea of travel has always appealed to me, so going abroad was one possibility. I did much research into the types of employment of which, for young people, dreams are made. All my application forms were completed but are now gathering dust on the window sill at home. Why, you may ask? Well, when I was served with my redundancy, I suddenly had a brain wave. Why not start my own business?

There is a definite trend in the market at the moment to set up new businesses. Whenever you turn on the television, the high street banks are advertising their help and support to people with enterprise. All over the country different organisations are cropping up, offering free help and advice to people like myself. Of course it was a very big decision to make. I was extremely lucky because I was only nineteen and had no mortgage hanging around my neck or other large financial commitments. The risk was definitely worth taking. I had to take numerous points into consideration. What was my business going to be, was my idea viable? I had the initiative and was fully committed but was there a niche in the market and did I need any training? There were so many things to consider that ideas were bursting out of my head.

The Employment Agency where I had been working provided a secretarial service to the public and a regular clientele had already been established. My business idea was to set up a company providing the same secretarial services for small companies, the general public and students. I was aware of some reasonably priced premises to rent in the city centre, an ideal location in the hustle and bustle of the growing commercial world. This golden opportunity was far too good to miss.

The first step was to seek professional advice, so I took a trip down to my local Enterprise Centre in Bradford. Whilst I was gathering brochures from their display stands I met a young gentleman who was absolutely bubbling over with enthusiasm. He immediately introduced himself to me as Previn Patel. I later discovered he heads the Enterprise Allowance Centre. He invited me to the University the following evening where an exhibition was being held for people who were setting up new businesses. The exhibition was my first major point of contact with many firms and individuals who have since provided me with invaluable help and assistance in my quest to become self-employed. I had no idea how many organisations there were which give free assistance for new businesses.

I had now established what my business was going to be and the next step was to produce a business plan and cashflow forecast. The business plan is a comprehensive report of the business idea, it is needed to show to your Bank Manager especially if you are applying for grants. It clearly indicates the short and long term objectives of the company and must illustrate the trader's personal capability of running a business. It is usually best to include a brief curriculum vitae. A copy of the cashflow must be included in the business plan and clearly justified, indicating where the figures were derived from and an allowance for contingencies has to be made — always be prepared for the

Mike Petty

worst! I had never come across either of these before and was definitely going to need assistance so I decided to see what courses were available to help me.

William Morrisons at Idle run a six week part-time course called Headstart in Business. The course is run by a trust, hence it is free for all attendants. The Morrisons Enterprise 5 course covers all aspects of starting and running a business, from book-keeping to marketing. On a regular basis the trust runs two courses, one full time course, consisting of sixteen weeks and another which is planned to help people who cannot attend in the daytime. This one is held on Saturday mornings and one or two evenings in the week. There are twelve sessions in all, each one being three hours long.

I then visited the Enterprise Agency. This was the first organisation to take a personal interest in my company. They took great care and attention over the financial aspect of my business, for instance they looked at how much capital the business was going to need, my personal requirements and my cashflow forecast.

To start the business plan I filled a scrap book full of different items which I was going to need to purchase for the business. Obviously for secretarial services, one of my main items was going to be a computer and printer. It is imperative to get several quotations for these as the market is very competitive and different products are available and not all will suit your exact requirements.

Week upon week was spent collating different quotations from suppliers but there are many other things needed apart from equipment, such as insurance cover, printing, stationery and a telephone. My rented office included electricity, lighting, heating and basic office furniture which reduced my costs. After many late evenings of work I was finally satisfied that I had chosen the best deals to suit my business needs. I put all the information down onto a cashflow projection. I also made sure not

Mike Petty

to forget to include a National Insurance stamp and an allowance for end of year tax. Initially I was going to be a sole trader. This is a far easier method from which to trade than the other alternatives.

My company would not be VAT registered, this only becomes a necessity when the business has a turnover in excess of £28,000 per annum. I did not anticipate this but realise that, once the company has become well established, becoming VAT registered and limited would mark a turning point in the success of my business.

Market research is imperative. I had always taken an interest in this but never had a chance to do some serious research. It is important to show that there is a need for your product or service, a niche in the market. I produced a questionnaire and distributed it amongst approximately 75 companies. I was delighted when 43 responded because it is usual to receive only a few back. The questionnaire indicated the kind of service my potential customers were most likely to use, which equipment they preferred and how often they were most likely to bring their work to me.

I then needed some statistics and graphs to show how many companies had started trading in the city over the past few years. The bulk of my business would be aimed at small companies who had a need for typed correspondence but could not afford a permanent secretary. I intended to display how many companies had started trading in Bradford over the past few years. This information was provided by Bradford Central Library, the Bradford Enterprise Agency and the Bradford Enterprise Centre, each one being extremely helpful and obliging. My business plan and cashflow forecast were now complete. It is always advisable to show it to professional people for their criticism, be prepared to rewrite it if any alterations need to be made. I knew that a bad business plan could lose me my business and I didn't want to be someone's girl typist all over again.

Looking for money

□ Enterprise is definitely a growing trend in Great Britain at the moment. So much so, that numerous associations provide grants and financial assistance for new businesses, these differ according to where the business is based, what the product/service is and the personal status of the trader. From what I could see I was entitled to apply for three grants, the first one being the Prince's Youth Business Trust which was set up by the Prince of Wales. Their support is available for people aged between 19 and 26. The charity helps people who have difficulty in finding any source of funding. They offer soft loans and bursaries of up to £1000. Unfortunately, because a bank had already expressed their interest in my business and had offered me the facility of a loan, the Prince's Youth Business Trust were not inclined to help my business. This is all very well but in my opinion the bank's extortionate interest rates are one of the reasons many small businesses fail in the early stages.

Another grant which I was entitled to apply for was the city's Business Start-Up grant. The grant can pay for office furniture, telephone installation and advertising. Unfortunately, when I applied for the funding for my business I was told that there was no money left in the kitty.

The final grant which I am entitled to apply for is the Enterprise Allowance Scheme. If you and your business fit certain criteria they give you £40 per week for your first year of trading. They hold business awareness days where you are made aware of all the ups and downs of being self-employed. Once you have attended on awareness days, you receive an A/Form, allowing you to apply. I am still waiting to hear from the Enterprise Allowance Scheme and have my fingers crossed!

Any grants should be looked upon as extra help and by no means the only source of money to be put into the business.

I needed a company name. The obvious names were AA Typing or A1 Typing, just so the name would be the first one in the Yellow Pages but I wanted something far more interesting. I decided I needed a name which conjured up an impressive image, one of professionalism and high quality. I wanted an object so I could have a small company logo and preferably an object of which the initial was one of the first five letters of the alphabet. I came up with *Diamond Secretarial Services* — a gem of a service!!

□ There's advantages in being a business woman and then there's disadvantages. On the plus side, as a team making independent videos which groups can commission for social purposes, we seem to get a lot of work from women's groups. I also know that when one Huddersfield based engineering firm bought in our services, the managing director had a sort of paternalistic attitude to us. He saw us as close to his daughters and was supportive in ways I do not believe that he would have been if we had been two slick young men.

On the other hand if David, my partner, is with us, because he is a bit older and a man, people tend to talk to him and want him to make the decisions. He understands my position and is supportive. He'll try to direct them back to me with eye movement and body language. Of course occasionally you need to be confrontational. We two girls once had it out with a couple of council officials who refused to treat us seriously and, in fact, were trying to get David to abandon us. We threatened them with Equal Opps. and they collapsed inward like a pack of cards. We didn't like doing that for generally the council is very supportive.

The other disadvantage is, because two women are involved, men come up and ask if it is a bluey, others hope it might be Candid Camera.

□ Since our business began, we two women have become interchangeable parents to our four children. They seem happy with this arrangement unlike my husband who has had to give up his rugby after twenty two years. He doesn't like looking after the children at the weekend.

☐ I needed start-up money so I went to the Listening Bank. "Listen", the manager said, "last year when you were on that textile vocational course in London, you ended up with an overdraft of £300. I'm sorry but you are a bad risk." That was a set back, I can tell you.

That needs some explanation. All the time I was doing a university course in Wales, my finances were well under control. I come from that type of working class background where you do not easily get into debt. London was different. Two of us were paying £100 a month for a room no bigger than a small front room and then there were all of the food costs. As well as doing a full time course, we were sewing in the evening and doing a job in a shoe shop on a Saturday, so we could not be accused of being lazy. London however is different, everything is so expensive. To have come away from Aberystwyth with nothing owing and to have had an overdraft of £300, when I think what some students have, is an achievement.

The Listening Bank didn't see it that way. So I changed my bank. Fortunately the assistant manager at Barclays was supportive. I had spent my final term of my college course doing an assignment which was a twenty page business plan and this impressed him. I had researched the area, costed equipment and materials, done a cash flow forecast and drawn up a marketing plan. It was nicely put together and that impressed him. He was prepared to give me an overdraft facility of £1000.

This was essential in getting the Enterprise Allowance money. I got another £1000 from the Prince's Trust and a second £1000 from Wakefield MDC Economic Development Unit. When it was put together — and the man at the Normanton Bank was very helpful there, doing a lot of phoning around to the agencies saying "If we put this in, will you guarantee your money" — I had enough to start up.

Just after I had won a prize for enterprise, the Midland Bank got in touch with me and said they would back me now. I told them where to put their money.

Rich man, poor man, beggar man

☐ Business families beget business women. That's because business sense in the family fuels the desire of the younger ones to follow in the footsteps of older sisters, brothers and parents. Basically you need a lot of confidence in yourself to start a business and to believe that you can succeed. If you've seen someone near to you manage things like going to a bank, or an accountant, then you will have a go.

☐ Most people are envious of someone whose parents have built up a good, solid business and then passed it on to their progeny, who take over and have it all on a plate. They obviously have to keep the business going but all the real work has been done for them.

☐ How helpful the banks are depends on whether you are a man or a woman. Black people have even more difficulty.

Two women were working in the same factory. One of them was asked by the local bus company to make head covers for the seats of his buses. The firm they worked for in the day was co-operative and they were allowed to use the sewing machines before 8 o'clock. Everything went well so they decided to go into business in a sheltered workshop. Since they had no finance behind them and they needed up front money, they went to the bank manager. He couldn't lend, although they would have been successful. His advice was "Sell your car." She couldn't, it was her husband's car. Would the manager have said that to a man?

It's also easy to forget the way people feel intimidated and made uncertain by solicitors and accountants.

☐ For the small business the biggest hurdle is finding an accountant who knows their business and will act for them at a small cost. There should be a new sort of accountant. It never crosses some accountants' minds to tell their clients how to save a few hundred pounds. Yet this is exactly what a small business woman needs.

☐ When I started up in business twenty years ago the banks were not a lot of help. If you think back to those times, banks looked like banks, places filled with mahogany and brass, and not like travel agencies as they do today.

They were conservative places and not community based. Of course the bank manager knew the local Freemasons, the members of the golf club and was involved in the local Chamber of Commerce, but he didn't know a lot about small businesses. Why should he? He was involved in non-risktaking enterprises.

When I called, my local manager wanted cast iron securities in the form of houses or an insurance policy. These are not the sort of thing you have in abundance at 22.

Now the wheel has gone full circle. Everyone is touting to lend money and the banks are looking for the small business man or woman. Some even have their own small business advisers, though I am still not sure if these people have the sort of expertise that is required.

☐ Although we have had money from the Prince's Trust and had a Wakefield MDC small business grant to set us up in equipent, we also have had practical support from our bank. We won a Barclay's Award for the "most innovative business idea in Yorkshire and Humberside" and this secured us a bank loan. They also gave us a filofax and an expensive brief case.

☐ Selling the idea to the bank was much easier than I'd imagined. I'd never had any dealings with a bank manager before. I thought he would look like Leo McKern but he was really laid back and swore.

I was wearing one of our shirts when we went to the bank, to display our product and the manager rang for one of the women cashiers to come through and have a look at it. She was middle-aged and not particularly fashionably dressed. He asked her how much she'd expect to pay for a shirt like mine. She said "About £25." As we were asking £30 for them I was really disheartened. Then he rang and asked a young lad of about 21 to come and have a look. He said he thought they were great and he'd be prepared to pay £50 - £60. That clinched it.

☐ Insurance companies are reluctant to insure computer software because the disks are vulnerable. I accept that, but what I cannot understand is how they can be so restrictive about other protection. I work from a room which has been tacked on to the back of my garage. It is fitted with burglar alarms, but to make it extra safe they are insisting that I put metal grilles up to my windows. At the moment the complete set up signals 'cowboy' and amateur, but the reality is that we are none of those things but rather a specialised operation which has decided to keep costs low by not taking on a 'city centre' office. Put up metal grilles at the windows and potential customers won't even bother to come inside the gate.

☐ I think that some people have an instinct about how to use money. I was always a saver. Even when I was a little girl I would have my Christmas orange well into the Spring. I don't mean a chocolate one, I mean a real orange. It's probably genetic.

Throughout my childhood I witnessed a lot of family arguments and the worst were always about money. I resolved that I would never be short. I've run a number of businesses but never failed though sometimes I have broken even.

Labour costs

☐ Ernie Precious — my wildlife mentor, sadly now dead — put me onto making

ornaments out of wood and pot birds. The nicest wood was yew with its lovely red colour. It would clean up beautifully after many hours with fine sandpaper and the final coats of polyurethane would vividly bring out the beautiful patterned grain in the wood. I had a supply of pot birds, tits, robins and wrens, which cost about a pound apiece. The bird was secured on a piece of dowelling, glued into the yew and fixed into a pleasing pose. I made quite a few of these ornaments, mostly giving them away as gifts to friends. People still say, "Oh I see you've got one of Tony's birds." My wife sold a few after people had seen them in my front window. I think the most I got for one was two pounds fifty pence.

One day Ernie and me were looking around York, the tourist paradise. In a specialist gift shop in The Shambles we saw a rough piece of silver birch, unpolished, with a porcelain bird perched on top. The bird was handmade by a chap in Harrogate and it was priced at £68. We looked at each other and smiled.

"Didn't we ought to be back in our shed making ornaments?" I said to Ernie.

"Not at £2.50p we didn't," said Ernie.

Natural walking sticks could have been my next business venture. I spent hours looking for perfect 90° handles on straight sticks. The kind we always wanted was a good handle and a honeysuckle perfectly spiralling down the stick and biting into the wood. I only ever found one.

To make the standard one the stick is left in a warm place to mature and dry out, then the handle is shaped and cleaned then polished. Finally the base is fitted with a copper ferrule and a broad headed nail to give a solid end. After four or five coats of varnish, the stick is complete.

A visit to any Dales Show would show the rough sticks with tin ferrules, one coat of varnish and priced at £9.50 each. They must have taken all of half an hour to make. So much for my walking stick business.

☐ Most people on the crafts side price themselves too low. They don't have any principles to go on and therefore they guess a price which makes little reference to anything except the cost of materials. They therefore sell when they shouldn't. On the other hand artists often price themselves too high.

A friend of mine who buys a lot of paintings says only a fool gives a painter what he or she asks. If you want to buy, knock the price down like they do in Eastern bazaars and also suggest that payment should be with three post-dated cheques. By this process he has become the first time buyer for a lot of new painters. They are happy, for if they had kept prices at the pitch they first offered them, then not much selling would have taken place.

☐ People talk about being a craftsman, but do not bother to go on and define it. I'll tell you what a craftsman is, a person who is making something that will support a way of life.

That definition of course removes from the equation almost everyone who sells at a craft fair. They are people who are indulging in a hobby or who are into the game for pin money. They start with a dream, a vision if you like, but never get beyond it into the hard world of making a living.

☐ It's easy to spend time talking to people without realising that time is your money. You need the customers' interest, but you cannot afford to let them spend too much time with you, especially as in most crafts, the profit margin is small.

It's interesting that people who have been serious craft workers, rarely talk when they see you working. They ration their questions and if they need to talk, buy something to compensate.

☐ I realised that I would never be a businessman because I didn't charge enough for my labours. I would charge for the tackle and add a bit on for the time, ignoring the use of my car and little things like screws and nails and clips. I could get more work than I really wanted but the few quid in my pocket was a small incentive to keep doing it. I worked for a contractor in Pontefract for a short while and had my eyes opened as to why contractors charged so much. They did charge for every screw and nail and every inch of cable. I would be told off for leaving six inches of cable too much at a socket, although it was charged for anyway. This was when I realised that business is business, nothing is for free.

☐ Many of my friends have often told me I ought to set up on my own and I obviously thought about it when I was particularly busy, but I realised that if I did I would have to start charging realistic prices for my work. I'd also have to have a van, another expensive item. I knew that most of my customers were word-of-mouth recommendations and if I charged shop prices they wouldn't need to come to me any more. Where was my trade then? These thoughts put paid to my business ideas. I'm really better off doing 'foreigners'.

☐ When people start up in business they never estimate their labour costs correctly. If they make walking sticks or pottery they can tell you to the last penny what the wood and clay costs. They might even be able to say what it costs to light and heat their place, but it is the unusual small business man or woman who is able to tell you what their hourly rate amounts to.

Why pay?

☐ You get all sorts of different ways of paying. Sometimes, someone who wasn't a regular customer, perhaps a farmer passing on his way to market, would bring in a broken implement, saying he'd pick it up on the way back. If it was just a small job it wasn't worth sending out a bill, so I would ask for payment straight away. Often they'd put their hand in their pocket, pull out some change and say, "Oh, I haven't enough on me, send us a bill". Then they would just ignore the bill, knowing they were not likely

Kevin Reynolds

to come back and you were not going to chase them for such a small amount. I got into the habit of having a quick look at what they had got in their hand and charged accordingly. That way at least I got something. I noticed they never pulled out their wallets.

Good regular customers would try to make you an offer, saying, "If I order eight, throw us in an extra one for nothing." But I could only make one item a day to order, so I couldn't afford to give one away. I was trying to compete against large manufacturers, hand-made against machine made; I couldn't even afford to charge a proper rate for my labour.

☐ As a teacher I had been involved in a bureaucracy and the freedom of getting up at five, loading up and watching the sun come up was heavy stuff. Mind, I didn't like the paper work and when people didn't pay on time I thought that was a personal affront.

☐ I was just packing up the other Saturday when three girls came up looking for fancy track suits. Although it was gone half past four I rooted round, found what they wanted and quoted the price, £32 a set, top and bottom. As I showed them I said, not aggressively, "They're a bargain, they retail at £60 in the big shops."

"That's not true," said one of the girls.

"Well luv," I said, "I won't argue with you. I've not seen them myself but that's what I have been told."

"No," she said, "I wasn't implying that you were lying. What they actually sell for in London is £79."

They paid with Access and Barclay Cards. Who would have thought that people would pay market traders with cheques, let alone plastic.

☐ What's an invoice? Now there's a difficult question for you. People ask for them and you are required to give them, but no one describes them accurately. In Sheffield Council, officers will only pass invoices if a VAT number is on the document. So in their terms an invoice is a piece of paper supplied by a business with a turnover of £25,000. Think where that puts artists and the like. Some of them won't do trade of £400 a year let alone £25,000.

Most, in their own homes, pay as many people as possible using dirty pound notes, and quite right too. Prices are based on that fact. Local councils don't get the benefits of that sort of transaction.

Plans as filing cabinets

☐ Business plans are like files. You take one out, add and replace it as the conditions change. The business plan is the filing cabinet. When you are bettering yourself and your business, you take down the business plan and modify it. It's not there to dictate action but to facilitate action.

☐ To run a business, you need to be very clear about your aims, and it helps to get these written down. When we started, our business plan was a page and a half for the bank. Now it's 38 pages on computer. Our long term aim is very clear. We would like to have 500 major museums around the world buying our jewellery. If they each sold three pieces a week that would bring in half a million. We've a bit of a way to go though; at the moment we have 12 museums.

☐ In the few months that I have been established, I have had to change my approach in the day-to-day management of my business. Now instead of saying "The waggon will collect the rollers," I try to transport as much as possible in the boot of the car. I like to know I have got my hands on the order.

I have had a few setbacks. I took on other products which looked good, but turned out to be a waste of time. I now consider it wise to give a product six months maximum and if there is a poor return, drop it. That's where the business plan is useful.

I would strongly advise anyone considering doing the same thing to make sure they have a sound business plan and keep a close check on budgets. You should build a margin to cover the unexpected. I built in a margin of 10%, it should have been 20%.

It is important to seek the advice of a good accountant and to make sure you take out a full life insurance cover of at least £50,000. In five years time I hope to be comfortably off, no more than that. Anything more will be a bonus.

☐ We've not done an analysis of who goes on the boat, perhaps we should. In the first year I suspect that about 70% was sunshine trade and about 30% booked in parties. Now the figure has reversed. That's good because we are not controlled by the weather.

☐ This man went on a Bradford training course for ten months and reckoned that he knew everything about business but we were more sceptical. When we asked him for a business plan he seemed surprised and when we offered him the chance to research one he promised to have a go, but spent the time making a promotional video. He got everything the wrong way round.

His plan was to set up a private ambulance service for Leeds but when we asked if he had any paramedical skills he said he hadn't. On pushing him a bit further, we also discovered that he couldn't even drive. "How did he see his position in the company?" was our final question. That he answered right away. He intended to be chief executive.

In the end it was apparent that he was not asking the primary question "What do I need?" but "What can I get away with?"

☐ It is also essential to see that before you go any further, you should prepare a business plan to prove profitability, present this to the bank and gain their approval and financial backing. I got the loan and bought the necessary equipment; a car, desk, answering machine, filing cabinet and, in my case that most essential aid, a car phone.

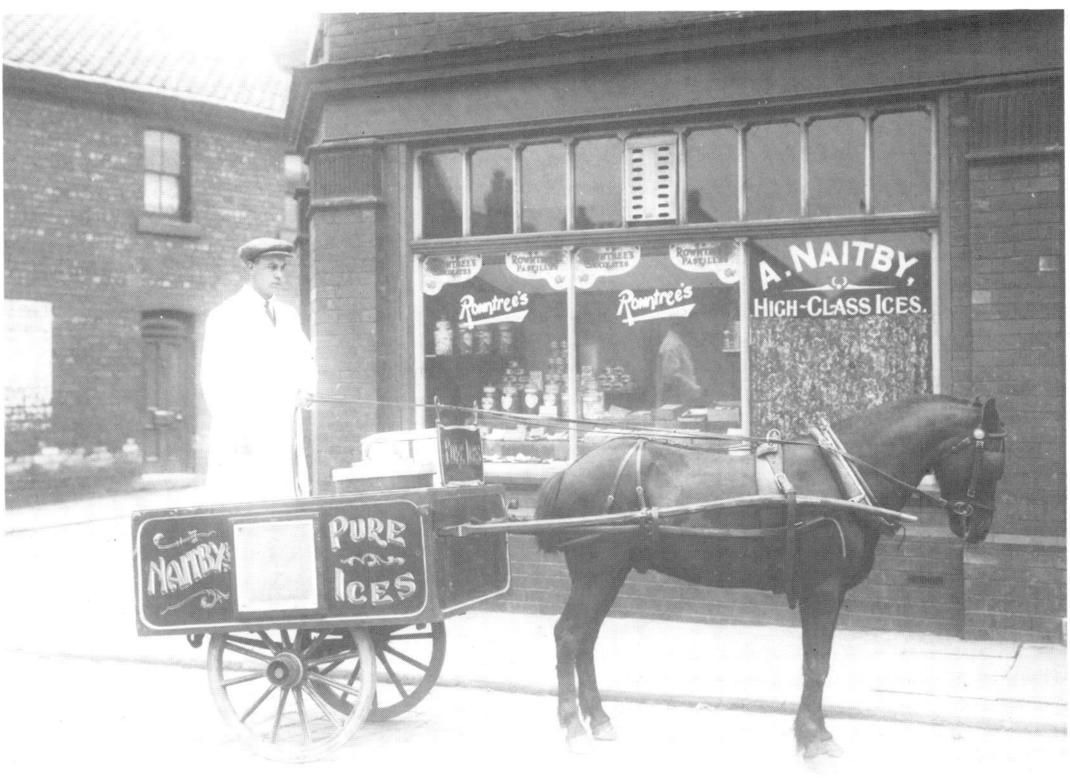

Mike Petty

I chose to stay in the roll-covering business because it seemed to be the sensible thing to do having twenty years experience behind me. With all my recent contacts, I had established my customer base at a stroke. Without that I could have spent months establishing one.

When I finally made the move from being employed to self-employed, I experienced a feeling of combined elation and terror. I had a family to support and a large mortgage. I knew the whole thing was a huge gamble, I must not fail.

Being self-employed makes you far more aware of tightening your belt, you also need an understanding bank manager. I obtained my finance from Lloyds Bank where I found their business manager very helpful. Lloyds have a business centre where they give free advice, they also issue an information pack.

☐ Some things have got better as time has passed. The four of us are communicating better and we've got better at organising our lives to meet deadlines. I still tolerate meetings rather than relish them and in any case we need them if we are to devise a strategy.

One advantage of trying to put together a business plan is that it focuses activity. You need to have thought things through and that in itself not only gives you business awareness but imposes a deadline. If you know you have to present a plan to a bank manager on a particular day, then you go ahead and work out a strategy.

☐ Right from the start we were told that we must get the perfect business plan to present to the bank. We spent night after night worrying over it. It was like doing our homework, but we still couldn't get it right. We had a preliminary meeting with the bank and the manager said to come back next week. I thought "God, I haven't got a business plan yet." But he said, "Never mind about that, just scribble something down."

Alligators and swamps

☐ Management is totally underrated. In this company there are two principal partners, both engineers. One, I'll call him George, said to me "It'll be good when we get there, I'm taking over the shop floor and Albert is taking on the management." When I talked to his partner he exactly reversed the situation; he was controlling production and George was to be the manager.

You can see why it happened. Both had come up through technical education and saw the world in those terms. Neither wanted management so they assumed that someone else would do it.

☐ If you haven't got a theory of management you'd best get one because if you try to do everything yourself you flounder. After a certain level of production has been achieved or the work force has grown beyond a certain point, you just have to delegate. That's a quantum leap for a lot of small business men/women. The wise ones realise that training isn't an extra, it is an essential. That's why anyone concerned about economic development pushes management training.

☐ It's all alligators and swamps. In most organisations the activists want to catch or kill the alligators whereas the real job is to drain the swamp.

☐ One firm sent a mail shot to America about their product. "If we get even one order" said the boss "I don't know how we will do it." There was no management there to cope with exporting. It was crazy really.

☐ A lot of men in small businesses reckon that where it's at is on the shop floor in the setting up of the machinery. That's the real job. The rest, clerical skills and management skills, is woman's work. Quality control will be valued but not much else is vital. When 1992 comes along and the horizons get broader, that sort of director is in for a rude awakening.

☐ We had been going for about three years when the situation got worse. On the surface we were on top of things but there was a great deal of tension. Key workers started to fall out, different styles were emerging. One of the partners, a woman, started to file everything, have fixed programmes and know everything that was going on. The other one wanted to have his own area of work and not keep any records at all. When pushed he said that it was better three years before when everything was played off the back foot and initiatives were seized on without a lot of discussion. It was exciting in those days.

One of the main people in the business, however, went in for reading and hit on a book which explained that what was happening was inevitable and that what they were experiencing was a common growth pattern. That came as a relief I can tell you.

The man was very appropriate for the first stage of any business; he was the classical pioneer. He'd work all hours God sent, find inventive ways of solving problems, go off like a rocket and get quick results. At the beginning he was an asset and without him there would not have been lift off.

The woman was more appropriate to the second stage of business development. She was a systems person and without her, the business was doomed to fail or stay small. Having got lift off it went beyond the pioneering stage and she was the consolidator who would nurse it into structured development.

When we saw what was happening and had all read the book, we didn't send the man off to the knackers' yard. What we did was to ensure that we recognised the value of the new procedures and kept him involved in those areas where he could pioneer to his heart's content without messing things up.

☐ A lot get it wrong and think that good management is a branch of the sciences whereas it is more closely associated with the arts. In business you often come at

problems which have to be analysed so quickly that it is sensitivity and emotion, qualitative judgement, which gets you through. You move instinctively and are in the end controlled by the finer nuances of a situation, not by a systematic analysis.

I don't, of necessity, employ graduates but people who can do the job. I know how to spot them, they are people who have flair. Now how can you quantify that: flair. Yet I can spot it.

That doesn't mean that I don't read; just the opposite. I'm fascinated by the culture of business and have well over two hundred books on management. I subscribe to the Harvard Business School for the periodical, but in the end it has to be an emotional grasp of a problem which finds expression in my enthusiasm.

That and being a workaholic.

☐ I have to admit that until very recently I underestimated training and business theory. I was prepared to let others in the organisation go on courses but, if I am truthful, I thought these were one up on expensive pleasure trips. I was content to do the work, let them get the theory.

My opinion altered dramatically when two of the women, having been on a three day course, came back and insisted not only on telling us about what they had done, but running a practical seminar on management structure. I went with some misgivings I can tell you. I had a lot to do that morning.

They said that there were four basic types of person in any organisation; the activist, the reflector, the pragmatist and the theorist. They explained each in turn and as they talked, I recognised that at least three of us fitted into these categories. Of course, none of us were wholly settled in one grouping, but there was something in the structure they described, to make me think this was not a load of bull. They acknowledged that you could not alter personality but you could modify management behaviour and achieve greater efficiency if the managers understood themselves and their relationship to others in the organisation.

Put in this way it sounds too simplistic by half, but as I sat there listening to two colleagues telling us what they had learned, I suddenly realised that what they were saying was true. I was essentially an activist and one of them was a reflector. The reason we got up each other's noses was not because either of us was inefficient; just the opposite, we were extremely efficient in totally different ways.

Literate but not literate enough

☐ We went to the top floor of the IBM building in Albion Street for a Seminar. The man who was giving it had offered it free as his contribution to arts development, he was an amateur dancer but also a business consultant. Later, one of the women said that she hardly recognised him without his leotard.

IBM does not quite have the look that the Midland Bank has; you know, women in clothes that you have paid for, but there is a corporate image and he had it; clean shaven, black suit, black tie and white shirt. He was exceptionally friendly though and clearly at the sharp edge of state of the art business technique.

The office was not like any office I had ever seen. It was where he worked yet there was no paper, no pens, no wall charts, no timetables, no books and definitely no filing cabinets. All there was was a keyboard and word processor screen. "Everything I need is in there," he said and to prove it, brought up the notes on our appointment and after we had finished, keyed in the central points of our discussion. It was a new world.

☐ I am the only one in the office who is not computer literate; a dinosaur if you like. I hang on and appear reasonably efficient because I carry most of my information in my head and I have been around a long time, but given ten years I, and my type of businessman, will be extinct.

☐ The problem with a lot of small

businesses is that they are buying in new technology but not training the staff to use it. Computer firms are having a bonanza. They can sell some people anything.

☐ I saw the Watergate film *All the President's Men* the other day. The office of the Washington Post looked so dated. It was filled with typewriters.

☐ The cordless phone is my pet hate. I was in my local the other day when a smart arse came in, sat himself by the bar and phoned in to his base. He was trying to get money from a customer and shouting things like, "Take him for two grand; can you hear me Gordon, take him for two grand". This went on for some time. The conversation constantly interrupted by, "Can you hear me, can you hear me?"

In the end two men got up — built like shit house doors they were — and went over to him. One, I remember, had concrete all over his boots.

"Aye, I can hear you," he said, "Now sod off."

☐ The difficulty is getting people to recognise the need to train and then finding the time to do it. You'll usually find the person who needs it most doesn't feel the need to go on a management training course.

As we came out of this course I heard this woman say, "Well I've learnt a lot today, but I guarantee that I shall have been so busy by four o' clock tomorrow making sausages, I shall have forgotten it."

☐ One of the principals in a major business training initiative came to see me. "I could do with a bit of training myself," he confided, "I don't know about spread sheets."

As I see it, the £40 ought to be linked to some employment training initiative of one or two years' duration, otherwise money is being thrown away. That, and seeing that the trainers are trained.

Short sighted, long sighted

☐ The Japanese say we have too many accountants and solicitors in our board rooms and when you think of it, there are more accountants per head of the population than engineers and that cannot be healthy. That we are good at financial management might be true but that's not what you need when it comes to innovation around a product. We have just not got the right trained people. We have emphasised the need for professionalism, said that is the in thing we need and consequently looked for management skills. You can see it in local government, there are very few trained managers. The way you get to the top is by being good at something; for instance, because you are a good solicitor, and as a result you don't get taught management skills from an early stage. You have to learn that being a good manager doesn't mean being the boss, with all that implies in terms of power, it means being something different. Knowing how to organise your own time efficiently and to recognise your goals. Managers should remember they are draining the swamp and not killing off the alligators that are attacking them.

☐ The Germans have a lot of engineers in top management. The same goes for the Japanese, and increasingly the French. We, by contrast, spend a hell of a lot of time checking figures instead of getting on with the job. Our goals are often different. British companies want to achieve more and more profit. The Japanese by contrast want to be well known. The British want a return in three to five years. The Japanese are prepared to wait twenty five years for their returns. The banks are often to blame for these short fuse objectives.

☐ I don't think we are efficient yet, but I do know this, that if we had been judged on three years' trading, we would have been classed as failing. It took us three years to learn from the mistakes, put the systems in place and come to terms with the language of the market place. We were not dunderheads but intelligent people, yet for all that, we had, until we started, been someone else's employees and the type of decision you make then is different from what you make when working for yourself.

☐ In Europe they believe in small businesses as a method of growth. It is recognised that big businesses grow from small ones and government policy is directed to insisting that the big companies support the little ones. Of course their time perspectives are different, much longer than ours; here people want to see an investment in three years. That is wholly unrealistic.

☐ Local government could help small businesses by looking for what can be found in the locality and buying from the local firm. They don't. They are too easily seduced by the glossy brochure and the packaging.

Councils are big spenders. How often do they deliberately set out to find out what their own have to offer? That's one way of making economic development happen.

I'll tell you what the difference is between this job and being somebody's employee. It's five minutes. In those days I had to be there for nine o'clock. Now I can be there at five minutes past. Mind I now work until midnight.